BERLIN AIRLIFT

BERLIN
AIRLIFT

ARTHUR PEARCY

Airlife
England

Copyright © 1997 Arthur Pearcy

First Published in the UK in 1997
by Airlife Publishing Ltd.

British Library Cataloguing-in-Publication Data
   A Catalogue record for this book
   is available from the British Library

ISBN 1 85310 845 6

MoD photographs used are British Crown Copyright and
reproduced with the permission of the Controller of her
Britannic Majesty's Stationery Office.

Typeset by Phoenix Typesetting, Ilkley,
West Yorkshire.

Printed in Italy

Airlife Publishing Ltd
101 Longden Road, Shrewsbury SY3 9EB, England

Acknowledgements

Many have contributed the hard core of facts on which this volume is based. While some kindly furnished contemporary letters and diaries or specially written accounts of their airlift experiences, others submitted themselves patiently to question and answer type interviews.

My grateful thanks to the following organisations whose members contributed items large and small: British Berlin Airlift Association; Berlin Airlift Gratitude Foundation (Heinz-Gerd Reese); 7350th Air Base Group USAF, Tempelhof; Royal Air Force Gatow; Berlin Airlift Memorial Luftbrücke Chapter, Rhein-Main, Frankfurt; Landesbildstelle, Berlin; Air Historical Branch (RAF), Ministry of Defence; Royal Air Force Museum, Hendon; Quadrant Picture Library; Burtonwood Association; USAF Office of Public Affairs, Arlington, Virginia (1/Lt Peter S. Meltzer USAF); Department of the US Navy, Naval Historical Center, Washington Navy Yard, Washington DC (Bernard F. Calvalcante); Douglas Aircraft Company, Long Beach, California (Harry S. Gann); Berlin Airlift Historical Foundation (Timothy A. Chopp); Berlin Airlift Veterans Association (Bill Gross); Records, Info & Support Services (RAAF) Canberra (David Wilson); Royal New Zealand Air Force Museum (Therese Angelo, Research Officer); Glider Pilot Regiment Association (L. David Brook); WINGS RAAF Association; South African Air Force Museum (Major Dave Becker); Military Aircraft Photographs (Brian Pickering); Aviation Photo News (Brian Stainer).

The following are just a few of the many individuals who contributed in one way or another: W.G. Ager and Ken Burton (GCA info); Gilbert W. Aspin (New Zealand); Peter Berry; Peter J. Bish; F/Lt Geoff Boston; Peter G. Cannon; Sq/Ldr Jack Clark (Operation 'Racehorse'); Roy Day; Aldon D. Ferguson; Jennifer Gradidge; Sq/Ldr H. Harvey; Helga Hellman, USAF; Robert Jackson; Delia Kennedy; Robert R. Lawrence (USA); Peter Leeds; Sir Peter Masefield; Air Chief Marshal Sir Nigel Maynard; R.H. Nichols; Merle Olmsted (USA); F/Sgt Geoffrey Paget; Doug Pirus (USA); Bruce Robertson; Dennis Usher; Sq/Ldr T. Winchcombe. RAAF contributors: John T. Callinan; Air Marshal David Evans; Sq/Ldr E.G. Ferguson; T.R. Fry AQM; Group Captain R.K. McLennan, Air Adviser, London; Sq/Ldr A.R. Middleton; WO R.G. Williams. RNZAF contributors: G. Allan, RNZAF Defence Staff, London; Charles Cook; Sq/Ldr Harrison PRO RNZAF; Wg/Cdr A.G.E. Pugh. SAAF contributors: Brigadier G.A. Hallowes, Defence Air Adviser, SAAF, London; Major-General Duncan Ralston. Fellow airlift historians Ronald M.A. Hirst (Wiesbaden), Wolfgang Julien Huschice (Montagnac, France), and Robert Jackson, author of the excellent book *The Berlin Airlift*, who loaned photos from his volume.

My renewed thanks to the Airlife team under Alastair Simpson, with Peter Coles as book editor and Rob Dixon in the book design section. Lastly to my wife Audrey who spent many hours proofreading and reliving her personal experiences in Germany as a NAAFI manageress at Lübeck and Travemunde during and after the airlift period.

Sincere apologies and thanks to anyone I have not mentioned who contributed to this tribute to a great humanitarian operation which must never be forgotten.

Arthur Pearcy
Sharnbrook, Beds
February 1997

Above: Fortunately Tempelhof, the huge pre-war air terminus for Berlin, was mainly free of World War Two bomb damage. It was built as the city's principal civil airport and its magnificent buildings remain today, as can be seen on this excellent aerial photo.

The main frontal structure was reputed to be the third largest building in the world, and its underground sections housed an aircraft factory and a hospital during World War Two.

(*USAF*)

Foreword

by the Governing Mayor of Berlin, Eberhard Diepgen

Berlin looks ahead and Berlin remembers

Berlin, for twenty-eight years the divided German capital, is growing at a rapid pace into a European metropolis. We Berliners are happy and thankful to have found our unity in peace and freedom. However, on our future path, we will not forget the route we had to tread, nor will we forget the friends who accompanied us on this way and helped us.

In 1998/99 it will be fifty years since the Soviet Union suddenly and brutally closed all the transport routes which linked the free part of Berlin to Western Germany; 'because of technical difficulties' was the succinct expression in a teleprint as they shut down road, rail and waterway connections to Berlin. The reply of the Western powers to this blockade was the historically unique, technically unbelievable airlift of Berlin. The provision from the air of a part-city in which about two million people had sought asylum after the horrors of the second World War was a logistical master performance and from a political point of view the hour when the Western alliance and Germany's ties to the West were born.

General Clay, who was the driving force behind the airlift, General Frank Howley and General William Tunner, the technical fathers of the airlift, earned the gratitude of the Berliners, as did thousands of pilots, radio operators, navigators, ground staff and volunteers who worked day and night for the airlift. Special thanks are due, however, to the men who lost their lives for the airlift, and their families. Seventy-eight pilots, radio operators, navigators or transport workers were killed in air crashes or loading accidents. Their names are engraved at the foot of the Airlift Memorial; Berlin will never forget them.

I am pleased that this book will inform posterity of the exemplary feats which were performed for this city at that time. The Berlin airlift is the historical example of success in overcoming aggression by peaceful methods if there is the political will and the military back-up. We remember this with gratitude on the fiftieth anniversary of the Berlin blockade.

Germany Remembers the Berlin Airlift 1948-49

Forty years ago, on May 12, 1949, freedom triumphed in Berlin.

On that day, the courageous and spectacular airlift of the Royal Air Force, together with the French and US Air Forces, and the perseverance of the Berliners finally broke the eleven-month stranglehold of the Soviet blockade. Every thirty seconds, a plane landed in West-Berlin carrying all necessary goods and materials, thus keeping the city free and alive.

On that day, great determination, the commitment to freedom, and solidarity prevailed over brutal repression. Thus, German-British friendship was truly sealed.

We, the government of the Federal Republic of Germany and the German people, remember those who lost their lives and reaffirm our gratitude to the British people.

The airlift will not be forgotten. It will always be a token of German-British friendship and partnership for the cause of British freedom, human rights and democracy.

HELMUT KOHL
Chancellor
of the
Federal Republic of Germany

HANS-DIETRICH GENSCHER
Minister for Foreign Affairs
of the
Federal Republic of Germany

Lest we forget. This item appeared in most of the national daily newspapers in the United Kingdom on the occasion of the fortieth anniversary of the lifting of the Berlin blockade by the Russians on 12 May 1949. The contents are self-explanatory and typify the gratitude shown, not only by the Berliners, but also by the Federal Republic of Germany today.

Foreword

by Air Chief-Marshal Sir Nigel Maynard KCB CBE DFC AFC
President of the British Berlin Airlift Association, ex-Commanding Officer No.242 Squadron, Avro Yorks.

In his foreword the Governing Mayor of Berlin describes how, nearly fifty years ago, the Russians closed all the land and water lines of communication between Western Germany and West Berlin and how, in spite of the problems, the 'part-city' was supplied by air, thus avoiding a hideously dangerous political situation.

With all this I agree, but I must make the point that it was only because of the work of RAF Air Commodore R.N. Waite, then Director, Air Branch of the British Control Commission in Berlin, that the airlift started at all. Waite was convinced, against most expert opinion, that the operation was feasible, and it was with the results of his detailed examination and his determination and perseverance that he was able to persuade General Robertson, British military governor and a disbeliever, to discuss the matter with General Clay. After reading and checking Waite's project General Clay, full of enthusiasm, put all his authority behind it and the British plan was adopted by the Allies. General Clay was indeed a great 'driving force' behind the airlift plan, as was the Commander-in-Chief RAF Transport Command, Air Marshal Baker, but Air Commodore Waite's determination not to be defeated from the start must never be forgotten.

While the Americans, with their much greater resources, ultimately lifted the greatest tonnage, the success of the airlift was the result of the combined efforts of the USAF, the RAF and the British civilian air transport operators who lifted most of the liquid fuel. Without the contribution of any one of these it is debatable whether or not the city of Berlin and the Republic of Germany would be reunited today.

17 April 1997

Contents

This immaculate Douglas C-47 Skytrain 43-49081 is permanently parked by the Berlin Airlift Memorial outside the USAF air base located at Rhein-Main, Frankfurt. The undercarriage is supported off the ground, and the transport is rumoured to be fully serviceable. It is named *The Berlin Train*. (*Berlin Airlift Memorial*)

Introduction

With so many books already written, and so much other documentation available on the Berlin airlift, compiling this volume has not been easy. Official papers confirm that the total blockade of Berlin commenced at midnight on 23 June 1948, and that the first train to mark the ending of the blockade reached Berlin-Charlottenburg at 5.32 a.m. on 12 May 1949. In between these two historic dates, unfortunately, there appear many wide discrepancies. With the onset of the fiftieth anniversary of the ending of the humanitarian operation, there is already forecast a flood of new volumes.

Within weeks of the blockade being imposed by the USSR, the Allies created an air bridge in the restricted airspace imposed by the three air corridors into Berlin. It won the battle of the hearts and bellies of 2.5 million Berliners. To supply a city from the air with the necessities of life, with food, clothing and heating fuel as well as work materials and even parts for the construction of a power plant, was a unique operation, both logistically and politically. When the airlift into Berlin began it was initially conducted in a rather carefree, almost haphazard way. One small room at Gatow had been set aside as the Ops Room. Towards the end of July 1948 the operational strength of the airlift was supplemented with a variety of aircraft and crews from Britain's air charter companies. For them the Berlin airlift meant fat profits and a valuable boost to their status and future in the world of civil aviation. The need for liquid fuel was acute in Berlin, and the commitment to supply this commodity was undertaken entirely by the British civil operators. Berlin also had a requirement for thirty tons of salt per day, but it was an extremely difficult item to handle. It was not only corrosive but tended to seep from its packages. Short Sunderland flying boats from the RAF and Short Hythes from Aquila Airways with their hulls treated to resist corrosion were utilised to carry salt.

With the increase in aircraft reinforcements it became apparent that more airfields would   be needed for the ever-increasing traffic. British and American engineer battalions, together   with German railroad experts, constructed special rail and road approaches and unloading facilities. At the same time the personnel of the mobile RAF Airfield Construction Wings were busy adding to existing runways and repairing the temporary pierced steel planking (PSP) runways and taxiways as required. In Berlin there was no superfluity of airfields to choose from; in fact there were two only, Gatow and Tempelhof. Despite the many improvements carried out at these two airfields they were still insufficient to handle all the traffic the airlift now involved. A third airfield was constructed at Tegel in the French sector of Berlin. It was built by the Americans and was constructed

Below: Unfortunately not a great deal is recorded on the success of the five Fairchild C–82 Packets employed on the airlift. Their load figures and flights do not appear to be available, but need to be added to the final CALTF figures for the operation. Depicted is C–82A 45–57791 being unloaded at Tempelhof. The spacious cargo compartment and clam-shell rear loading doors, often removed for convenience, were ideal for airlift requirements for transporting heavy construction equipment etc. (*68365 AC Douglas*)

with German labour, much of it female, working round the clock for DM 1.20 per hour plus a hot meal every shift. The new airfield gave a much-needed increase to the tonnage that could be flown in.

Runway space was only one requirement of the huge humanitarian operation. Even more important was the Air Traffic Control and navigation aid equipment in use, and its operators and technicians. The bulk of the flying took place in the bad weather winter months with aircraft density at its highest. The schedule at Gatow was to land one and dispatch another every three minutes day and night – a movement in and out every ninety seconds. In the worst weather it could be stretched to five minutes. The airlift airfields possessed the latest ATC equipment, manned by highly skilled operators. Without these aids and the specialists to operate them, the transports could only have operated in good weather.

The work done on the ground, though far less spectacular, was just as important to success. There were the military and civil organisations who

Above: A four-year-old girl resident in one of Berlin's western sectors collects her family's bread ration from a bakery near her home. The bread was baked from American flour airlifted into the city, and is wrapped in a Soviet-licensed newspaper which carries a banner headline reading 'AIRLIFT USELESS'.
(*68216 USAF Douglas*)

Below: After the Russians blockaded the city of Berlin, refusing to allow supplies to be brought into the German capital by road, rail and canal, the huge airlift began with RAF Dakotas flying in supplies to Gatow and the USAF operating the Douglas C–47 equivalent into the airport at Tempelhof. Four-power control in the city was completely broken by the Russian authorities refusing to sit on the Berlin Kommandatura. Depicted during the early days of the airlift, on 1 July 1948, some twenty Skytrain transports are seen unloading supplies at Tempelhof. The second C–47 is 43–15284 and carries the livery of the European Air Transport Service (EATS) which was retained in Europe after World War Two.
(*BER 674665 Douglas*)

decided what commodities were necessary to sustain the existence of West Berlin. The planning of commodity supplies was the responsibility in Berlin, on a tripartite basis, of the three Allied commanders. In the bipartite office in Frankfurt these requirements were communicated to the various authorities involved, including HQ Staff of the British Army of the Rhine (BAOR), plus a special unit, the British Army Air Transport Organisation (BAATO). The latter was responsible for a 'seek and find' operation for the necessary goods wherever they could be obtained, to be despatched to the airlift air bases in the western zones of Germany. On each base the Army deployed units which stored, graded and checked the freight. They became specialist units manned by officers and men of the Royal Army Service Corps (RASC) supported by vast teams of German labourers. This was the Rear Airfield Supply Organisation (RASO). Gatow had a similar organisation known as Forward Airfield Supply Organisation (FASO).

The high degree of inter-Allied co-operation which developed was possibly one of the most noticeable features of the whole airlift operation. Drawing on the experiences of World War Two, the extent of effective collaboration soon surpassed all previous standards. On any given day at the Berlin airfields could be found aircrew from the US Air Force, US Navy, RAF, RAAF, RNZAF, SAAF and even the odd crew from the RCAF in Canada. Between these respective national air arms there was nothing but healthy rivalry, with nothing but respect for one another and the task in hand. It was a common goal.

Initially a plan was put forward to ensure the British troop garrison in Berlin remained fed and watered by airlifting in supplies during Operation 'Knicker'. The records show that on 12 April 1949 RAF Dakotas from Lübeck commenced to airlift the 1st Battalion Royal Welch Fusiliers, complete with goat mascot, to Berlin to relieve the 1st Battalion Norfolk Regiment. A month later on 12 May the Lübeck Dakotas commenced to airlift the 1st Battalion Gordon Highlanders to relieve the 1st Battalion Worcestershire Regiment.

Behind the scenes a great deal of research and development was conducted to improve the airlift, especially in the delivery of that very vital commodity coal. The staff with General Curtis LeMay envisaged a non-stop daily drop from the bomb bays of USAF Boeing B–29 Superforts, followed by an all-night floodlit operation in which gangs of workmen would clear the coal, but the first trial drop was a dismal failure and the coal inside the sacks was reduced to useless dust. In the UK during July 1948 at the RAF Central Bomber Establishment they carried out experiments in dropping sacks of coal from Avro Lincoln bombers. It was neither necessary nor a success.

Below: Clarence the camel, along with 7,000lb (3,175kg) of candy, was flown into Tempelhof in this C–47 Skytrain transport on 22 October 1948 as a gift for the children of Berlin. The baby camel was the mascot of the 525th Fighter Squadron based at Neubiberg air base in Germany. 1/Lt Don Butterfield was offered the small animal at Tripoli, Libya for $50. It was flown to Germany in the bomb bay of a Douglas B–26 Invader bomber. When Berlin was besieged it was decided to present it and the candy to the children in Berlin. (*Merle Olmsted*)

Above: Two RAF Fitter 2Es seen working on an airlift Dakota's Pratt & Whitney R–1830–90C Twin Wasp engine which developed 1200hp. The standard RAF Dakota had a three-bladed Hamilton Standard 3E50 propeller driven by 16:9 reduction gear. During World War Two with nearly 10,000 transports built – nearly 2,000 going to the RAF – the Twin Wasp was sub-contracted to motor manufacturers such as Buick. Photo taken at Fassberg.
(*R1769 MoD AHB*)

In the beleaguered city, the sense of solidarity was evident everywhere. Berliners gathered by the fences surrounding the old Luftwaffe barracks at Gatow, clapping and cheering as the four-engined Yorks taxied in. Many of them brought gifts for the aircrew. On 19 July 1948 when an all-RAAF crew flew a No.242 Squadron York loaded with 1,600lb (723.8kg) of flour from Wunstorf, little did they know this was the RAF's 3,000th sortie since the airlift began. Fräulein Gretel Schoenrock and her welcoming committee of pretty blondes from the economic division at Wiemersdorf City Hall kissed and embraced F/Lt J.G. Cornish, the captain of the York. In addition to the enormous bouquet of roses she presented a letter which read: 'Long live democracy. Long live freedom. May this small talisman [a tiny winged wooden horse] accompany you on all your flights and bring you good luck'. On the streets surrounding Tempelhof often up to 10,000 men, women and children lined Berlinerstrasse, bordering the busy airfield, perched in the forks of trees and on the rubble remains of ruined houses, waving from parked cars and trucks.

During the winter when the temperature often dropped to minus thirty degrees, the endurance and solidarity of the Berliners were admirable. To a large extent they were fortified in their resistance by the visible success of the airlift. When it was all over, an exhausted yet exultant Ernst Reuter, Mayor of Berlin, summed up the magnitude of the

Below: Originally a Halifax bomber squadron during World War Two, No. 77 Squadron flew Dakotas in India. On 1 December 1946 it took over No. 271 Squadron and was based at Manston, Kent when the airlift commenced in June 1948. On 8 November it was moved to Oakington, Cambridgeshire with its Dakotas where they joined the huge pool of transports operating out of Lübeck. Depicted is Dakota C IV KK128 YS–U, the No. 77 Squadron code, parked on an apron somewhere in Germany. The squadron was disbanded after the airlift on 1 June 1949.
(*R.H. Nichols*)

Above: Well over 200 Douglas C–54 Skymasters were employed on the humanitarian airlift of 1948/49. The transport first flew on 14 February 1942 and was built in quantity for the USAAF and the US Navy, being designated R5D– by the latter service. By the end of World War Two 839 C–54s were in service. In 1948, when called for service on the airlift, Skymasters appeared in the livery of a variety of commands including Military Air Transport Command (MATS), Air Transport Command and various US Troop Carrier Squadrons etc. Depicted are three USAF C-54 Skymasters parked at Rhein-Main air base. (*USAF*)

Allied achievement when he said: 'Without the bold initiative and admirable devotion of all those who created the airlift and co-operated in its development, Berlin could not have withstood the pressure; it would have disappeared into the Soviet zone. The consequences for the whole world would have been incalculable.'

The airlift had cost the lives of thirty-nine British and thirty-one US aircrews, as well as nine civilians. In monetary terms it had cost the United States $350 million, the United Kingdom £17 million, and the German people 150 million Deutschmarks.

The airlift provided the beleaguered city of Berlin with all the necessities of life for the population of an estimated two and half million who were completely isolated by the Russian blockade. Fresh milk is seen being unloaded from a USAF transport aircraft by German labourers. (*67615 AC USAF Douglas*)

Two RAF Fitter 2Es, including a WAAF, are seen working on replacing a fairing on the tail of an Avro York used on the airlift. Production of the transport for the RAF totalled 208 which included five VIP passenger transports, 114 pure freighters and sixty-four passenger/freighter versions. During the humanitarian operation the York carried 230,000 tons (234,000 tonnes) of supplies into Berlin in 29,000 sorties.
(*R1841 MoD AHB*)

Above: On arrival at Tempelhof air base Sergeant Poole, one of the crew of the C–54 Skymaster, supervises the unloading of his aircraft. Usual unloading time was twenty minutes. After this was completed the transport had to be inspected for potential sources of any engineering problems. Finally he hopes to grab a sandwich and cup of coffee before take-off. His twenty-four-hour shift means four round trips to Berlin with little time for eating, and no time for sleeping.
(*67809 ACUSAF*)

Below: On 13 September 1948 the first three of five twin-engined Fairchild C–82 Flying Boxcars arrived at Wiesbaden to supplement the airlift. The new transports were used for heavy, bulky cargo which could not be conveniently carried in other airlift aircraft. They were useful in the building of Tegel, airlifting large construction equipment which often had to be cut up with acetylene torches at Rhein-Main then welded together again at Tegel. Depicted is a C–82 making the first visit of the type to Tempelhof.
(*68364 AC USAF Douglas*)

Above: Avro York aircraft parked at their airlift base at Wunstorf; those carrying the 'KY' fuselage code are from No. 242 Squadron. Other York squadrons involved included Nos. 24, 40, 51, 59, 99, 206 and 511, while Yorks from No.241 Operational Conversion Unit (OCU) were also used on the airlift. The first twelve Yorks of RAF Transport Command arrived at Wunstorf during the evening of 1 July 1948 under the command of Wing Commander G.F.A. Skelton. (*AP Photo Library*)

Left: 'Wads and char' – the Cockney phrase for sandwiches and tea, seen being served from the mobile NAAFI van at one of the RAF airlift bases in Germany. The recipients of the all-important life-saving nourishment are from the GCA radar units seen in the background. During the airlift the NAAFI provided food and drink, cigarettes etc. around the clock.
(*R1816 MoD AHB*)

Below: The USAF 317th Troop Carrier Group equipped with the C–54 Skymaster since 1947, was busy flying courier and passenger routes to Japan, Guam, Korea and the Philippines when it was alerted for airlift duty in Germany. In September 1948 it transited, via the USA, to Wiesbaden, moving to Celle on 15 December. It had three active squadrons – 39th, 40th and 41st. Its motto was 'I gain by hazard'. Seen parked on the pierced steel planking area at Celle are a number of the Group's Skymasters. (*Doug Pirus*)

Above: A Rolls-Royce Merlin engine for an airlift Avro York transport being manhandled aboard Dakota C IV KN274 of the 'Plumber Flight' based with No. 58 Maintenance Unit (MU) at Honington, Suffolk. Spare wheels are also ready for loading. Day and night this unit, with its fleet of six Dakotas, supported the airlift bases in Germany with spares as required. (*R2104 MoD AHB*)

Right: Depicted at RAF Celle are two C–54 Skymasters from the 317th Troop Carrier Group which completed its last airlift sortie to Berlin on 31 July 1949. Also based in the British Zone was the 60th Troop Carrier Group at RAF Fassberg. It was activated in Germany as part of USAF (Europe) on 30 September 1946 equipped with the C–47 Skytrain and was involved in the early days of the airlift from Wiesbaden. Its four squadrons re-equipped with the C–54 Skymaster and moved to RAF Fassberg to continue supporting the airlift. (*Doug Pirus*)

Below: It was fortuitous that both the US 60th and 61st Troop Carrier Groups were based in Germany with USAF (Europe) and equipped with the ubiquitous Douglas C–47 Skytrain transport when the airlift commenced in 1948. Both groups later re-equipped with the C–54 Skymaster continuing on the airlift. Initially over 100 C–47 Skytrains were the mainstay of the US supply train into Berlin. Depicted is a USAF C–47 on final approach to an air base in Germany. (*Peter M. Bowers Collection*)

The Blockade Begins

On 31 March 1948 the Soviets issued an order requiring personnel and baggage on military trains to and from Berlin to be checked by their inspectors. All freight on military trains departing Berlin could not be cleared unless a permit was obtained from the Soviet commander in Berlin. Both General Lucius D. Clay, Commander-in-Chief of the US Forces in Europe and Military Governor of the American zone in Berlin, and General Sir Brian H. Robertson, British Commander-in-Chief in Germany and Military Governor of the British zone in Berlin, were determined to challenge the Soviet orders. Clay was authorised to reject the new Soviet regulation and to send US military passenger trains through the Soviet checkpoints. The guards were instructed to prevent Soviet military personnel from entering the trains.

Three US military trains entered the Soviet zone during the evening of Monday, 31 March. One train commander lost his nerve and permitted

Below: The first military governors of occupied Germany, including Berlin, were the three victorious Allied combat commanders – Zhukov, Montgomery and Eisenhower – who soon delegated deputies. The US named General Lucius D. Clay, on 15 March 1947, as Military Governor and US Commander-in-Chief in Europe. He was a professional officer and engineer with high political connections, and until his departure in May 1949 he was America's proconsul in Europe with almost unlimited authority. He took steps to strengthen US forces in case the Berlin crisis developed into World War Three. (*via Robert Jackson*)

Soviets to board the train which was allowed to proceed to Berlin. The other two trains were stopped, but the Soviets were denied entry. They had the train shunted to a siding until morning when they were backed out to the US zone. Two British military trains were treated similarly. So as not to acquiesce with the Soviet orders, Clay cancelled all US military trains to and from Berlin, and laid on an airlift. This became known as the 'Little Lift' and lasted initially from 2 to 4 April but no longer than ten days. The US Air Force in Europe (USAFE) had twenty-four serviceable Douglas C–47 transports at Rhein-Main, Frankfurt, and they flew in about 300 tons (305 tonnes) of supplies for the military garrison in Berlin, but there was no provision for the civilian populace of the city or even a thought of attempting such an operation at that time. The Soviets eased their restrictions on Allied military trains on 10 April, but continued periodically to interrupt rail and road traffic during the next seventy-five days.

On 5 April a major incident occurred in the air corridor to Berlin when a Soviet Yak–3 fighter aircraft first buzzed and then collided head-on with a scheduled British European Airways (BEA) Vickers Viking G–AIVP to Gatow in the British sector. Both aircraft crashed, killing the Soviet pilot and fourteen passengers plus crew in the Viking, including two US citizens. The Russians claimed the British airliner had violated air safety regulations and was to blame for the accident.

During April and May instances of interference on the land and water access routes into Berlin increased again. Between 1 and 4 June several mail trains were left standing at the zone border. On 15 June the autobahn bridge across the River Elbe at Magdeburg was closed. Despite a detour over an improvised ferry, road traffic was hindered rather than helped. In the middle of this confusing situation, shortly before midnight on 23 June the lights went out in Berlin. The Soviets had cut off the electricity from the gigantic power plant at Golpa-Zschornewitz, which for decades had supplied the city with power.

On 23 June the Department of the US Army officials in Germany read a grim message from General Clay: 'US military freight train was stopped at Marienborn at approximately 0500 hours 21 June. Train was not allowed to proceed to Berlin due to refusal of train commander to permit Soviets to open cars for inspection. At approximately 1700 hours 22 June Soviets took over train under threat of arms, attached Soviet control locomotive to train and sent it back to Helmstadt – all under the strong protest of our train commander . . .' The intentions of the Soviets were clear. To force the Allies out of Berlin and end what they termed 'Western interference', they would plunge Berlin deep into isolation by cutting its power and food supplies, barring the waterways, blockading the roads and, hopefully, destroying the people's will to resist.

General Lucius D. Clay, after taking advice, ordered the start of what was to become the Berlin airlift. Before the Russians lifted the blockade on 12 May 1949, thousands of tons of food and supplies had been delivered in history's greatest air transport effort. Seventy-nine American, British, French and German fighters died to keep a city alive. Their struggle is an eternal symbol of the human will for freedom.

Those of us who know freedom must keep it forever alive. The Berlin airlift was mainly about liberty, about the West Berliner's right to freedom and to choose the way of life he or she wanted.

Frau Louise Schroeder was Berlin's first female governing mayor who during her term of office laid the foundation for a rationing system more equitable and more efficient than the Germans had known for a long time. She saw it as her main task to make the winter of 1947/48 less horrible for the people of Berlin than the preceding winter had been.
(*via Robert Jackson*)

By October 1948 the governing mayor of Berlin was Ernst Reuter who helped the Berliners to survive the blockade, predicting that they were prepared to make sacrifices for their political freedom. He had been arrested by the Nazis in 1933, released in 1934, and emigrated to Turkey where he worked as a school teacher and an official of the Ministry of Economics. He arrived back in Berlin during January 1947 and became a spiritual leader of Berlin during the airlift.
(*via Robert Jackson*)

Below: It was Douglas C–47 Skytrains from the 60th Troop Carrier Group which carried the first relief supplies into Berlin in June 1948 when the blockade commenced. The unit was reactivated at Munich on 30 September 1946, moving later to Kaufbeuren and then to Wiesbaden for the duration of the airlift. Many C–47s from the widely based European Air Transport Service (EATS) were also impressed into airlift use. Shown here is C–47A–80–DL 43–15221 parked on the apron at Tempelhof.
(*R.H. Nichols*)

Below: Air Commodore J.W.F. Merer RAF, Air Officer Commanding the British Forces on the humanitarian airlift, is seen with Major D.M. van der Kaay of the South African Air Force. Air Commodore Merer became deputy to Major-General William H. Tunner USAF, Commander of CALTF with HQ at Wiesbaden, but as Air Officer Commanding No.46 Group RAF Transport Command he chose to retain his headquarters at RAF Bückeburg.
(*R2002 MoD AHB*)

US President Harry S. Truman was one of a group of five who decided to mount an airlift to Berlin. Along with Prime Minister Clement Attlee, Truman was a decision-maker; neither could be bothered with detail. Having decided on a course of action they expected that it would be carried out. Truman's stance over the Western Allies' rights in Berlin, and against the spread of communism in Europe, was unwavering.
(*via Robert Jackson*)

On 15 October 1948 a Combined Air Lift Task Force (CALTF) was established at Wiesbaden. Its commander was Major-General William H. Tunner USAF, one of the architects of US air power, who during World War Two was in charge of the massive airlift of supplies from India to China over the 'Hump'. On 26 July 1948 'Bill' Tunner had been appointed to command Operation 'Vittles' by the USAF Chief of Staff.
(*via Robert Jackson*)

Clement Attlee, who had succeeded Winston Churchill as British Prime Minister, and along with Foreign Minister Ernest Bevin, apparently acted quickly to get the British air supply operation into action. The speed with which the British government reacted to the Berlin crisis even surprised the Americans.
(*via Robert Jackson*)

At the Foreign Office Ernest Bevin succeeded Anthony Eden as Foreign Minister. Bevin had enjoyed considerable success in the wartime Cabinet as Minister of Labour and he had had a long experience in combating communism in the pre-war trade union movement. He was one of the few diplomats who declared his faith that the airlift would succeed.
(*via Robert Jackson*)

Below:
Seen in the markings of 46 Squadron RAF XK–Y Dakota KN518 c/n 33058 is parked on an airfield in Germany. This transport took part in the humanitarian airlift and was one of eighty-nine Dakotas overhauled by Airwork at Eastleigh. After RAF service it was returned to the USAF as 44–76726, in 1953 going to the French Air Force, and it ended its military service with the French Aéronavale. A survivor today, it was last reported at Palma, Majorca registered EC–EQH but withdrawn from use. (*Peter Berry*)

Below: On 1 July 1948 for Phase II of the Berlin airlift the first Avro Yorks were flown from bases in the United Kingdom to RAF Wunstorf, Germany, and two days later were engaged on the airlift. Of the forty Yorks available, it was planned that thirty would be operating at any one time, flying a daily total of 120 sorties. At the end of the airlift the Yorks had contributed 233,145 tons (236,875 tonnes). Shown parked at RAF Gatow are Avro Yorks engaged on the airlift. (*Sqn Ldr H. Harvey*)

Above: German workers unload vital sacks of flour from a USAF Douglas C–47 Skytrain transport at Tempelhof, Berlin. Coal represented two thirds of all tonnage airlifted into the city, but bread was the 'staff of life' even though it was rationed. (*USAF A83–12–2 via Douglas*)

Above: Fuel hauling presented a major problem initially. At first fifty-five-gallon metal drums were used, as shown here being unloaded from a USAF C–47 transport. This method proved unsatisfactory with the necessity of steam cleaning the empty drums and airlifting them out of Berlin. A contract was awarded to Flight Refuelling for the services of a fleet of Avro Lancastrian tanker aircraft capable of delivering 550 tons (558 tonnes) of liquid fuel a day. (*67614 AC USAF Douglas*)

Above: A variety of USAF C–47 Skytrain transports seen parked on the loading ramp at Rhein-Main in preparation for another supply flight to Berlin. The ubiquitous 'Gooney Bird' transport was impressed from units far and wide within the USAFE operational area. Many still showed signs of their involvement in World War Two.
(*67703 AC USAF Douglas*)

Above: Today this Douglas C–47 Skytrain 45–951 together with a Douglas C–54 Skymaster is preserved at Tempelhof Airport, Berlin as a tribute to the transports which were involved in the humanitarian airlift in 1948/49. The transport carries the livery of the European Air Transport Service (EATS) which operated throughout Europe after World War Two and was one of the earliest post-war transport units to be based at Tempelhof in 1945.
(*USAF Berlin*)

Right: Berlin children watch from wartime rubble as a US Air Force C–47 Skytrain climbs out of Tempelhof air base on 5 July 1948 after delivering vital supplies. The type was the only one available when the crisis broke out in June 1948 and was succeeded by the larger C–54 Skymaster.
(*Landesbildstelle-Berlin*)

Above: Between 2 and 4 April 1948 some twenty-four USAF Douglas C–47 Skytrain transports operated 'Little Lift' from Rhein-Main, Frankfurt into Tempelhof with roughly 200 tons (203 tonnes) of supplies. It was extended but lasted only about ten days' flying with approximately 300 tons (305 tonnes) of supplies for the military garrison in Berlin. Shown here are C–47 transports unloading supplies at Tempelhof in heavy rain. (*67610 AC USAF Douglas*)

Right: USAF C–47s from Rhein-Main unloading supplies on the apron at Tempelhof. (*Landesbildstelle-Berlin*)

Below: The transport aircraft in most common use on the airlift during 1948 was the Douglas C–47, known as the Dakota by the RAF. A rugged and durable transport, it had been the aerial general factotum as used by the Allies in World War Two and it equipped the USAF, the RAF and the French Air Force at the time of the airlift. Unfortunately it was capable of only lifting a mere 6,000lb (2,722kg) of payload, which was simply not enough to meet the escalating needs of Berlin under siege. (*AP Photo Library*)

Top: Initially the RAF Douglas Dakota and the USAF equivalent the Douglas C–47 Skytrain managed the massive airlift. On 26 June 1948 thirty-two C–47 flights from Wiesbaden airlifted eighty tons of supplies into Tempelhof. At this time the USAF had available fewer than 100 C–47s, mostly from the European Air Transport Service (EATS). Shown here is an impressive ramp shot taken at night as a C–47 is parked with its load of vital supplies. (*AP Photo Library*)

Above: The first RAF aircraft on the humanitarian airlift was a Dakota from No.18 Squadron, the crew being Pilot 1 B.G. Hughes, Nav 2 S.A. Botsford, and Sig 2 K. Driffill, the date 26 June 1948. This photo shows the crew sat on the wing of the Dakota which is appropriately inscribed. The original requirement for Operation 'Knicker', later 'Plainfare', as given in No.46 Group Ops. Order No.7/48 dated 19 June 1948 was a daily airlift of 130,000lb (58,967kg). (*RAF Museum P1168*)

Organisation and Operations

Apparently there was a wide divergence of opinion among the American, British and French officials about the feasibility and desirability of remaining in Berlin, and almost universal disbelief that the city could be totally supplied by air over an extended period of time. Although both US and British political and military leaders immediately stated their forces would remain in Berlin, they were not at all certain they could or, if they could, for how long. The British Labour government was in agreement with General Clay's views on remaining in Berlin, but the French foresaw grave problems and notified Clay: 'The French government is obliged to dissociate itself from all responsibility with regard to these consequences.' In spite of this rebuke, the French went along with all major decisions made by the US and British governments during the Berlin crisis of 1948/49.

In June 1948, the US Army and the US Air Force in Europe, as elsewhere, were mere skeletons of the huge well equipped forces of World War Two. The huge demobilisation of 1945/46 and the end of all military draft in 1947 left only a volunteer US Army in Europe of approximately 60,000 men. The US Air Force had become independent on 18 September 1947 and had a few tactical fighter squadrons and miscellaneous aircraft based in Germany. It had two troop carrier squadrons equipped with the ubiquitous C–47 which were used to ferry personnel and supplies. These were the only aircraft in USAFE capable of hauling cargo. The British Air Forces of Occupation were in a similar plight with only three squadrons of fighters. Back in the UK, airmen due for demobilisation were surprised when told their service was extended for a further six months. Veteran aircrew flew home from overseas ready to settle down in civvy street while thousands of aircraft, including RAF Dakotas, were put into storage at maintenance units scattered around the UK. The poor French had almost no aircraft at all to offer. The odd Junkers Ju 52/3m, a few Dakotas and a few Flying Fortress bombers were used as transports.

General Sir Brian Robertson, British Commander in Berlin, suggested to General Clay that he considered the possibility of supplying Berlin by air, and he had already secured agreement for the RAF to start supplying the Berlin garrison. The British government was also considering

Above: Fortunately RAF Honington, Suffolk, had been a Transport Aircraft Modification Unit (TAMU) since 1946, specialising in the Dakota. Depicted is the 'nerve centre' of the unit, which during the Berlin Airlift organised the requirements for the RAF squadrons based in Germany and engaged in supplying Berlin with its needs. Its fleet of six Dakotas, known as 'Plumber Flight', flew a supply link as required day and night. *(R2106 MoD AHB)*

Above: During the airlift, RAF Gatow in the British sector of Berlin became one of the busiest airfields in the world. This photo shows the ever-busy Operations Room at Gatow with the Wing Commander Flying, Wing Commander T. Piper, talking to the Station Commander, Group Captain B.C. Yarde, who is seated. Based on the estimated tonnage of 480 aircraft landing in any twenty-four-hour period, major improvements were made to the airfield. By the time the last official airlift aircraft, a Hastings, had landed on 6 October 1949, more than 110,000 landings had been made at Gatow. (*R1822 MoD AHB*)

supplying the civilian population of nearly two and a half million by air, but Clay was not certain such a plan could be carried out effectively. While looking at alternatives he called in Ernst Reuter, the mayor-elect of Berlin, who was accompanied by his aide, Willy Brandt.

Only one known source has revealed that the original idea for the airlift project was not American (through the offices of General Clay) but was the concept of a senior RAF officer, Air Commodore R.N. Waite, Director, Air Branch with the British Control Commission in Berlin. Apparently some forty-eight hours before the Soviet blockade came into effect, Waite had alerted RAF Transport Command HQ to the probability that 'some form of airlift' into Berlin would be required shortly. On 23 June 1948 he submitted a rough plan for an Anglo-American airlift to sustain Berlin to Major-General Herbert, Commander of the British sector of Berlin, only to be informed it was out of the question. Not to be outdone, Waite engaged himself for many hours with a slide-rule, calculating cargo priorities, theoretical availabilities and load factors of transport aircraft. He returned to Herbert the following day with a more detailed logistic plan complete with figures, requesting just ten minutes with General Sir Brian Robertson. After looking the plan over and doubting that it

was possible, he agreed to show the proposals to General Clay later that day. The result was nothing but enthusiasm for the project and, after a second look, Clay instructed General Curtis LeMay, USAF Commander in Germany, to take all one hundred or so Douglas C–47 Skytrains from all other tasks and employ them on flying supplies into Berlin. Twenty-four hours later the first C–47s arrived at Tempelhof. The date was Saturday, 26 June 1948, although General Clay in his memoirs states that the first C–47 specifically with German cargo arrived in Berlin on 25 June.

It was a worrying time for Clay, who estimated that the maximum that could be expected was 700 tons (711 tonnes) a day, and he knew from his planners this was far short of the minimum to sustain the population of the western sectors of Berlin. No one was thinking, at this time, of an airlift operation lasting more than a few weeks. On 26 June, Clay's decision was supported by President Truman at a cabinet meeting in Washington, against the advice of some of his counsellors. He ordered the airlift to be put on a full-scale organised basis and that every transport aircraft in the European Command be made available; the European Air Transport Service (EATS), for instance, a transport unit formed in Europe after World War Two whose C–47 transports and crews were detached on VIP and logistics missions far and wide within the theatre, soon had its war-weary Skytrains pressed into airlift services. Like many others, Truman was thinking of the airlift as a temporary measure because after making this decision he stated, 'In this way we hoped that we might be able to feed Berlin until the diplomatic deadlock could be broken.'

Clay was also supported by two important US individuals who were in Europe on an inspection tour when the Berlin blockade began. William Draper had been Clay's economic adviser in Berlin prior to becoming US Army Under-Secretary so was familiar with the food and other supplies requirement necessary to sustain the city. General Albert Wedemeyer had been US Army theatre of operations commander in China during World War Two when Allied aircraft flew over the 'hump' from India with supplies. It was coincidental that the 'hump' operation had been commanded by one General William Tunner who was later to head the Berlin airlift operation. Both Draper and Wedemeyer recommended that supplies by air to Berlin be initiated, and on 24 June Draper recommended the USAF be requested to move additional transports to USAFE command.

The British Foreign Secretary, Ernest Bevin, a strong advocate for remaining in Berlin, obtained British Parliament support for basing Boeing B–29 Superfortress bombers in the UK, and argued that the airlift should be built up immediately to 2,000 tons (2,032 tonnes) per day. When General Robertson informed General Clay of this British support, the latter sent the following cable on Sunday, 27 June to William Draper:

I have already arranged for our maximum airlift to start on Monday (28 June). For a sustained effort we can use seventy Dakotas (C–47s). The number of which the British can make available is not yet known, although Gen Robertson is somewhat doubtful of their ability to make this number available. Our two Berlin airports can handle in the neighborhood of fifty additional airplanes per day. These would have to be C–47s, C–54s, or planes with similar landing characteristics as our airports cannot take larger planes. LeMay is urging two C–54 groups. With this airlift, we should be able to bring in 600 or 700 tons (610 or 711 tonnes) a day. While 2,000 tons (2,032 tonnes) a day is required in normal foods, 600 tons (610 tonnes) a day (utilising dried foods to the maximum extent) will substantially increase the morale of the German people and will unquestionably seriously disturb the Soviet blockade. To accomplish this, it is urgent that we be given approximately 50 additional transport planes to arrive in Germany at the earliest practical date, and each day's delay will of course decrease our ability to sustain our position in Berlin. Crews would be needed to permit maximum operation of these planes.

Below: Fuhlsbüttel was the civil airport serving Hamburg and was under the control of the Civil Aviation Control Commission of Germany. As a Berlin airlift base the airfield facilities were improved and included the construction of a new 5,850ft (1,783m) concrete runway. New airfield lighting and apron facilities were also added. Shown is the scene during a meteorological briefing for some of the many civil aircrew who operated a wide variety of aircraft, including Handley Page Halifax/Halton transports, these being the first civil type to be based at Hamburg. (*Tony Smith*)

Above: RAF Wunstorf was the initial airlift base for the RAF Dakotas, which moved on 29 July 1948 to Fassberg; when the USAF moved in with C–54 Skymasters on 22 August, they moved to RAF Lübeck, constructed in 1935 and used post-war by the RAF as an Armament Practice Camp. As with other bases involved in 'Plainfare' Lübeck required extensive expansion, runway extension, a large hardstanding and a parking apron 88,000 square yards (73,576m²) in area. It had a railhead capacity which was doubled. A concrete road was laid to the huge bulk fuel installations, covering an area of 4,000 square yards (3,344m²). New airfield lighting was installed plus adequate lighting for the huge parking apron.

Emergency meetings were held on both sides of the Atlantic. Truman approved a British request for joint military planning and a joint Anglo-American military meeting was held on 30 June. The US Secretary of Defense was James Forrestal, and the USAF Chief of Staff General Hoyt S. Vandeberg. Here in the UK Chief of the Air Staff was Air Chief Marshal Sir Charles Portal – he, along with General Albert Wedemeyer, was a man of great distinction. The man they later appointed to run the airlift – General William H. Tunner – was their chosen technician, the Western world's supreme air transport specialist. The deliberations were conducted with great care and attention to detail for probably at no time in post-World War Two history, with perhaps the exception of the Cuban missile crisis in 1962, has the world ever been closer to World War Three than it was during the period from 25 June through to late July 1948. After receiving the go-ahead from General Clay by telephone on Friday, 25 June, General LeMay gave immediate orders to the 60th and 61st Troop Carrier Groups' HQs at Rhein-Main and Wiesbaden to commence flying in supplies to Berlin. The following day C–47s were able to fly in eighty tons of supplies. General LeMay appointed Brigadier-General Joseph Smith from his staff as project officer for the US component of the airlift.

Naturally, when the airlift began the organisation was makeshift but enthusiastic. Airlift crews of the USAF had an original name for Operation 'Vittles' – 'LeMay Coal and Food Company', in honour of the airlift's organiser. Captain Arthur Eve Jr USAF was the Chief of Personnel Operations for the 7100th Support Wing, 7120th Air Base Group (ABGRU), at Wiesbaden, the HQ of USAFE. He recalled:

Above: All airborne activity was centred on Air Traffic Control and the station briefing room was manned night and day. Shown in the Lübeck briefing room is ACW Delia Thompson with the map showing the three corridors in/out of Berlin. (*Delia Kennedy*).

When the airlift started, 'desk' pilots assigned to staff jobs at USAFE Headquarters, Wiesbaden Military Post, European Air Transport Service, augmented the two troop carrier Wings to provide around the clock flights. My assignment was to furnish German nationals as loading crews. It was Saturday, 26 June, the day after the blockade started. Fortunately, the standard work week for German nationals was six days, so it didn't take long to round up enough people to start.

It was coincidental that the airlift occurred almost simultaneously with major changes taking place in the US military air transport system. On 1 June 1948 the new Military Air Transport Service (MATS) was formed, consolidating USAF Air Transport Command and the US Naval Air Transport Service (NATS). There was an interval of a few months before the NATS units would be completely merged into MATS, and in that interim period US Navy air transport assets were controlled by Fleet Logistic Support Wings.

When the call went out in late June 1948 for Douglas C–54 Skymaster transports, the first units called on to supply aircraft were the 20th Troop Carrier Squadron, Panama Canal Zone; the 54th Troop Carrier Squadron, Anchorage, Alaska; the 19th Troop Carrier Squadron, Hawaii; and the 17th Air Transport Squadron, Great Falls, Montana. Other C–54s came from Bergstrom AFB, Fairfield-Suisun, California, and Brookley AFB, Alabama. By 10 July some fifty-four C–54s had arrived to supplement the C–47s.

It was a telephone call from the Air Ministry in Whitehall, London, to RAF Transport Command Headquarters located at Bushy Park, near Teddington, Middlesex, in the early hours of Saturday, 26 June 1948 which set into motion the biggest and most important peacetime air operation ever undertaken by a single command of the RAF, and one equal to many of the most hazardous undertaken in war. From Transport Command HQ Order No.9 was issued on 30 June 1948 to reflect a Cabinet decision. It stated, uncompromisingly:

1. Following the breakdown of the surface communications between the British Zone of Germany and the British Sector in Berlin, the latter will be supplied completely by air.

2. The airlift into Berlin to be built up as rapidly as possible to 400 tons (406 tonnes) per day and maintained at that level until 3 July 1948. Therefrom it is to be increased to 750 tons (762 tonnes) per day by 7 July 1948.

3. In Phase I up to 3 July inclusive, Dakotas of No.46 and No.38 Group operating under the control and direction of Air Headquarters, British Air Forces of Occupation (Germany), will provide the 400 tons (406 tonnes) per day lift.

In Phase II they were intended to be supplemented by the four-engined Avro Yorks from No.47 Group.

The airlift was given overriding priority over all other Transport Command operations. It involved the cessation of all training and the cancellation of most of the worldwide scheduled services. It was hoped that the increase to 750 tons (762 tonnes) per day would coincide with the completion of the new runway at RAF Gatow. The original requirement for

Right: RAF Honington, Suffolk, had been in use by Transport Command since early 1946 as a maintenance and spares base mainly for RAF Dakotas. During the airlift six Dakotas known as 'Plumber Flight' flew spares as required to Germany. Vehicles were also included and the station became the vital 'hub and spoke' supply system for airlift spares etc. This photo shows Wg/Cdr H. Foreman OBE, Chief Technical Officer, on the left being briefed by the Senior Engineering Officer Sq/Ldr James Taylor OBE. (*R2102 MoD AHB*).

Operation 'Knicker' was given in No.46 Group Operation Order 7/48 dated 19 June 1948 which called for a daily lift of 130,000lb (58,967kg) for the maintenance of the British forces garrison in Berlin. This lift required twenty-four Dakota sorties daily, and was estimated to last at least a month.

A conference was called by the Air Officer Commanding (AOC) No.46 Group, Air Commodore J.W.F. Merer, of all station commanders and officers commanding the technical Wings located at RAF Waterbeach, Oakington and Bassingbourne. A far larger effort was envisaged involving the transport aircraft from both Nos.38 and 47 Groups. A new codename, 'Carter Paterson', was chosen which early in July became Operation 'Plainfare'. Dakotas from Nos.46, 53, 77 and 238 Squadrons were positioned at Wunstorf along with Dakotas from No.240 Operational Conversion Unit (OCU) and began airlifting supplies into Berlin. The first twelve Avro Yorks arrived at Wunstorf on 12 July under Wing Commander G.F.A. Skelton. On 19 July the small Transport Wing HQ formed at Wunstorf was disbanded and replaced by Transport Operations at the Schloss at Bückeburg, HQ of the British Air Forces of Occupation. When 'Knicker' had been planned it was envisaged that two RAF air movements sections would be capable of handling the limited amount of freight and passengers airlifted each day; however, the magnitude of the task soon proved to be far beyond the capacity of the RAF air movements organisation and on 28 June an HQ Army Air Transport Organisation (AATO) was formed by the HQ British Army of the Rhine at Wunstorf, later moving to the Schloss. A

Rear Airfield Supply Organisation (RASO) at Wunstorf and a Forward Airfield Supply Organisation (FASO) at Gatow appeared. It is estimated that the Royal Army Service Corps (RASC) controlled 1,500 lorry movements per day.

On 22 September 1948, an advanced operational headquarters from No.46 Group HQ in the UK was detached from Transport Command to Germany. Its task was to take over executive control of all airlift operations involving British aircraft. The advanced HQ comprised a skeleton staff including signals, navigation, air movements and aircraft control plus technical staff and a small administration liaison element. The new AHQ was located in the Schloss, Bückeburg alongside HQ AATO and absorbed the Transport Operations room.

On 15 October 1948 discussions between HQ BAFO and HQ USAFE resulted in the establishment of a Combined Air Lift Task Force (CALTF) at Wiesbaden. Its commander was Major-General William H. Tunner USAF with deputy Air Commodore Merer, the AOC No.46 Group who remained at Bückeburg with his headquarters.

The role of No.38 Group Transport Command was to reinforce No.46 Group with aircraft and personnel, requiring the bulk of the training programmes to either cease or be drastically reduced. The demand on No.38 Group resources resulted in the disbandment of two squadrons, but at the same time in August 1948 Nos. 47 and 295 Squadrons were ordered to re-equip with the newly introduced Hastings aircraft. The first squadron arrived at Schleswigland on 1 November and the first flight to Berlin was accomplished ten days later.

Below: Normally based in the Panama Canal Zone with the 20th Troop Carrier Squadron, 314th Troop Carrier Group, this C–54, 43–17223 is seen being loaded at Rhein-Main in preparation for a flight to Berlin. There had been no time wasted in flying the four-engined transports over to Germany, and no time in which to eliminate any unit identification. (*AP Photo Library*)

Above: Passengers from Berlin disembark from an RAF Dakota on arrival at Lübeck. No fewer than nine squadrons of RAF Dakotas were involved in the airlift, these being Nos. 10, 18, 24, 27, 30, 46, 53, 62 and 77. No. 240 Operational Conversion Unit (OCU) based at Dishforth, Yorkshire, was also involved, contributing both aircraft and aircrew. (*AP Photo Library*)

Above: The Avro York freighter with its large fuselage loading doors proved its worth during the airlift. Depicted is York MW232 being unloaded with parts of a steamroller vital for airfield rebuild and maintenance. On 17 December 1948 this York MW232, piloted by F/Lt Beeston, airlifted a cargo of canned meat into RAF Gatow. It was the 100,000th ton (101,600 tonne) of provisions flown in during Operation 'Plainfare'. Frau Louise Schroeder, the Deputy Mayor of Berlin, was at Gatow to receive the incoming York and its cargo with due ceremony. (*R1849 MoD AHB*)

Below: The first twelve Avro Yorks for the airlift arrived at Wunstorf on the evening of 12 July 1948 under Wing Commander G.F.A. Skelton. Initially they operated at a maximum loaded weight of 60,000lb (27,216kg). On 16 July the landing weight was increased to 65,000lb (29,484kg) and the maximum take-off weight went up to 67,000lb (30,391kg). These Avro Yorks are lined up at RAF Gatow unloading vital supplies for Berlin. The first aircraft is MW271 from No.24 Squadron and it carries the radio call-sign 'MOYD–X' on the nose cone. In the background can be seen Gatow Air Traffic Control with Station HQ behind. (*Quadrant Picture Library*)

Above: Even prior to the airlift British European Airways had operated a daily passenger and freight service into Gatow. Passengers were normally carried in a Vickers Viking airliner from Northolt via Hamburg, while freight was carried in one of BEA's fleet of Douglas Dakota transports. Shown on the apron at Gatow during the airlift is a Dakota G-AJIV unloading freight parked next to a VIP RAF Dakota KN645 carrying insignia on the fin, identifying it as the personal transport of Field Marshal Bernard Law Montgomery, one of the four Allied Commanders in Europe. (*Landesbildstelle - Berlin*)

Right: Surrounded by airlift personnel, including US Air Force and British civilian aircrew plus German labourers, and with a US Air Force Douglas C–54 Skymaster parked in the background, Air Marshal T.M. Williams, AOC-in-C British Air Forces of Occupation (BAFO) since 1948, signs a huge airlift anniversary card. Air Marshal Williams shared the higher command of the Combined Air Lift Task Force (CALTF). (*AP Photo Library*).

Below: On 17 August 1948 a Douglas C–74 Globemaster I made its first internal airlift flight after arrival from the USA. It arrived at Rhein-Main three days earlier with eighteen spare R2000 engines and parts for the C–54 Skymasters, the load weighing 85,000lb (38,556kg). It carried twenty tons (20.3 tonnes) of flour – twice the normal C–54 payload – into RAF Gatow. In this photo crews take a break while the elevator of the C–74 lifts over four tons (4.07 tonnes) of flour into the cabin at Rhein-Main. (*68072 AC USAF Douglas*)

Below: The first RAF squadron of Transport Command to be equipped with the Hastings C1 transport was No.47 based at RAF Dishforth, Yorkshire, in October 1948. A month later it was based in Schleswigland, Germany, flying industrial coal into Berlin. It was later joined by No.53 and No.297 Squadrons also equipped with the Hastings. Here coal is being loaded into Hastings TG572 at Schleswigland by German labour (*CHP1595 MoD AHB*)

Above: RAF Transport Command Avro York MW105 'K for King', the first pure freighter York built, in No.241 OCU markings, trundles down the taxiway at Gatow. It is being followed by an Airflight Avro Tudor 2 G–AGRY which served the airlift as a freighter prior to being converted to a tanker. The York was powered by four 1,620hp Rolls-Royce Merlin engines while the Tudor 2 had four of the more powerful 1,750hp Merlin 102 engines. (*RAF Gatow*)

Above: Three of the five Fairchild C–82A Packet transports assigned to the airlift on 13 September 1948 have been identified as 45–57740, 45–57791 and 45–57818. The latter is seen parked on the apron at Tempelhof being loaded with some unusually unwieldy and heavy equipment, possibly required for the construction of the new Berlin airfield at Tegel. In most cases, while operating on the airlift the rear double loading doors were removed. (*Landesbildstelle – Berlin*)

Airlift Bases

As more and more tonnage was flown into Berlin, it became necessary to increase the number of bases. At the peak of airlift operations nine bases in West Germany were operational, all airlifting into three airfields in Berlin. A look at the three air corridors into Berlin showed that the central and northern corridors from and to the British zone were not only shorter, but at a lower level above sea level than the southern corridor leading into the US zone. By October 1948 the airlift was utilising six British zone airfields – Bückeburg, Fassberg, Fuhlsbüttel, Lübeck, Wunstorf and Schleswigland – with a seventh nearing completion at Celle plus the old Blohm & Voss seaplane base at Finkenwerder. Only Wiesbaden and Rhein-Main in the US zone were being used.

The British, who operated a mixed fleet of both military and civilian contract transports, could not fully use their better sited airfields. The US, who by October had standardised their aircraft fleet with the larger C–54s, capable of delivering a ten-ton load per aircraft, were supplying more than 3,000 tons (3,048 tonnes) per day plus the 1,500 tons

(1,524 tonnes) per day by the British, so it was logical to base as many C–54s as possible at the RAF bases, where the transports could do the work of three from Wiesbaden or Rhein-Main. When Celle was completed in December, General Tunner moved in C–54s in addition to the ones already operating out of RAF Fassberg. Lübeck became the receiving station for 68,000 persons, mainly children and elderly folk evacuated for some reason from Berlin and selected by the Berlin City Health Department, while Bückeburg operated a courier passenger shuttle to and from Berlin and a similar service to and from the United Kingdom.

November, December and January were notorious for providing some atrocious weather conditions. Germany lies on the same line of latitude as Labrador and its mean temperatures are similar to those of the US mid-Atlantic coast, so it presented one of the most difficult weather forecasting areas in the world. The North Sea is one of the coldest, and in winter the proximity of the warm Gulf stream causes an intermixture of air masses of widely varying temperatures and humidity, with frequent frontal passages making

Opposite: By 10 July 1948 over fifty Douglas C–54 Skymasters had arrived in Germany to supplement the C–47s. They came from units far and wide after an order from General Clay to bolster the aerial Berlin lifeline. Shown on arrival at Rhein-Main is a C–54 from the 9th Air Force based at Greenville in South Carolina, whose insignia is beneath the cockpit. (*67954 AC USAF Douglas*)

Below: Despite the continual flow of daily flights, full-time labour was employed to keep the runway at Tempelhof and other air bases in good order. Here a grader is seen at Tempelhof as a USAF C–54 Skymaster comes in to land. By July 1948 the combined US–British tonnage being flown into Berlin was averaging 2,500 tons (2,540 tonnes) in over 600 daily flights. However, it was still some 4,500 tons (4,572 tonnes) short of the figure envisaged by the planners as a daily minimum requirement. (*68642 AC USAF Douglas*)

Above: When airlift pilots were on final approach to Tempelhof they looked down upon many roofless fire-blackened ruins. It was ninety minutes by air from the USAF airlift base at Rhein-Main/Frankfurt. This huge air terminus had been designed prior to World War Two as Berlin's civil airport and, as can be seen from this photo, it had some magnificent buildings in its design, including a massive operations and administration block with at least seven storeys underground. When the USAF took over the air base following a brief Soviet occupation, engineers laid a 4,987ft by 120ft (1,520m by 36m) runway, together with a large apron and connecting taxiway built of concrete block. At the commencement of the airlift US engineers warned that the single runway would not last more than sixty days under the heavy pounding of loaded aircraft.
(*68183 Douglas*)

weather prediction, timing and forecasting a major problem for the US 18th Weather Group, which had a squadron serving the airlift in Europe and another in the United Kingdom. Each base had a US weather detachment. The US Air Force Air Weather Service (AWS) had a squadron of WB–29 weather observation aircraft based at Burtonwood while a squadron of WB–17 Flying Fortress aircraft operated out of Wiesbaden on weather observation missions. Airlift pilot reports were used extensively; a change of a single degree in temperature or a change in wind force and direction could mean the difference between a successful landing or a missed approach and return to base.

When the Combined Air Lift Task Force (CALTF) was set up in October 1948 it made available in December to all its pilots a manual 60–1 entitled *Airlift Routes and Procedures* which not only contained the standard operating procedure (SOP) chart for all the airlift bases, but the instrument approach charts for twenty-six bases in Europe to be used in case of diversion. One C–54 loaded with coal managed a missed approach at Tempelhof due to low cloud and reduced visibility, and on its return down the corridor to base the pilot learnt that the weather had gone below landing minima. The Skymaster plus coal finally landed at Marseille (Marignane). Each aircraft had to be equipped with the appropriate VHF radio crystals for each base, just in case.

The French had a lack of transport aircraft in Europe, so were unable to do a great deal to support the airlift. At this time they had heavy political commitments in Indo-China where most of the Douglas C–47 Transports of the Armée de l'Air were deployed. (The Armée de l'Air did operate out of Wunstorf early in the airlift period with three Junkers Ju 52/3m transports. Unfortunately this undertaking came to an abrupt end when two of the three-engined Junkers crashed into each other and were totally destroyed while taxying at Wunstorf. The French withdrew as not much could be achieved with the one remaining airworthy transport.) However, in December 1948 they did demonstrate they were willing to contribute. It had become clear that the freight centres at Gatow and Tempelhof were too small for the huge volume of cargo being flown in daily in order to keep Berlin alive. A third Berlin airfield was desperately needed and a site was found in the Wedding suburb located on the Tegeler-See in the French sector which had been used during World War Two as a training ground for Luftwaffe air defence divisions and which now lay wasted. The new Tegel airfield was completed on Friday, 5 November almost two months ahead of schedule. However, before it could become fully operational a 200ft (61m) radio tower obstructing the approach and owned by the Soviet-controlled Radio Berlin needed to be removed.

Numerous French requests to the Soviets to dismantle it had been ignored. Early in December the French attached explosives to the base of the tower and blew it up.

By late summer 1948 the airlift planners decided that a form of advanced training was required for aircrew and even maintenance personnel prior to assignment to Germany. The USAF moved the Military Air Transport Service (MATS) school from Fairfield-Suison AFB – now Travis AFB – California to Great Falls, Montana, during September 1948 and established a 'Vittles' training operation. Hundreds of pilots and crew were checked out on the C–54 aircraft and flight procedures for corridor operations into Berlin. They had mock-up duplicates of the facilities at Rhein-Main, Wiesbaden and Berlin so that both ground and flight procedures could be simulated.

It was 1934 when the Nazis first cleared the trees and hillocks of the Ritterfeld, as the woodlands around Gatow were known. To the south, adjoining the airfield, they built a flying school. No expense was spared and the entrance complex was particularly striking. The long building containing the arch of the main gate curved purposefully like a buffalo's horns towards the road outside. Beyond that, across the Kladow road on the shore of the Havel lake, similar buildings appeared for a luxurious staff college and technical school. Luftwaffe Gatow was a prestigious project on the edge of the first city of the Third Reich – Göring boasted of it and in November 1935 the Führer himself opened it.

In April 1945, in the last hours of the war in Europe, the hardened soldiers of the Soviet 47th Army poured across the western airfield boundary. Gatow became a Soviet airfield for two months, the only RAF station with such a pedigree. On 25 June 1945, amid the ruins of a defeated Germany, a line of vehicles from 2848 Squadron RAF Regiment snaked its way from Magdeburg to Gatow to stake the RAF's claim to the airfield. On 1 August 1945 Royal Air Force Unit, Berlin, became RAF Gatow. In 1947, as if forewarned of the events of the following year, the British embellished their new grass airfield with a concrete runway.

The huge air terminus in Berlin, Tempelhof, had been designed before World War Two as the city's principal civil airport, and it has some magnificent buildings, including a massive operations and administrative block with at least seven storeys underground. During the war years this remarkable structure, reputed to be the third largest building in the world, housed, among other things, a factory producing Focke-Wulf Fw 190 aircraft and a well-equipped hospital. When the USAAF took over the airport following a brief Soviet occupation with Yak–9s of the 515th Fighter Air Regiment, and later by units of the 193rd Fighter Air Division, they laid a 4,987ft by 120ft (1,520m by 36m) pierced steel planking (PSP) runway, together with an apron and connecting taxiway built of concrete block. When the first Americans moved into Tempelhof on 2 July 1945 they were confronted with many problems due to extensive damage and pilfering. On 1 September 1945 control was taken over by the European Air Transport Service (EATS) equipped with C–47 Skytrain transports which

Below: It was 8 October 1948 when the decision was taken to open Schleswigland in northern Germany as a base to accommodate RAF Hastings transports. It was 6 October 1949 when the type flew its last sortie having contributed no fewer than 55,095 tons (55,977 tonnes) to the humanitarian airlift. With Hastings parked on the taxiway, German labour is depicted busy extending and strengthening the airfield. (*R2044 MoD (AHB) via Bruce Robertson*).

later, in June 1948, helped to initiate Operation 'Vittles'. Two additional runways were constructed at Tempelhof during the blockade; the first was completed in September and the second in October 1948.

The USAF began the airlift with the advantage of having an established air base at Rhein-Main near Frankfurt which had been developed after World War Two as a vital gateway to Europe for both civil and military operations. A Luftwaffe base during World War Two, it was largely destroyed by Allied bombing. In 1948 it was the European terminal for the huge US Military Air Transport Service (MATS). The resident unit was the 61st Troop Carrier Group with its three squadrons – 14th, 15th and 53rd – equipped with the C–47 transport. Rhein-Main had a 6,000ft by 150ft (1,829m by 46m) runway which was to prove adequate for airlift operations until early 1949 when the tempo was increased. A new runway 7,000ft by 200ft (2,133m by 61m) was commenced but it was only twenty per cent complete when phase-out of the airlift began.

Wiesbaden was the other principal air base in Germany which was also HQ USAF (Europe). It had been a Luftwaffe fighter base and in 1948 the resident transport unit was the 60th Troop Carrier Group with three squadrons equipped with the C–47 Skytrain. In April 1948 it was this group which carried out the mini-airlift to Berlin with supplies for the garrison. It became home of the 1st Airlift Task Force under General Curtis LeMay, later becoming HQ Combined Air Lift Task Force (CALTF) under General William Tunner with effect from 15 October 1948. It then became home to C–54 Skymasters under the 7150th Composite Wing. General Tunner noted that the American corridor from Wiesbaden and Rhein-Main into Tempelhof was half as long again as the other two corridors. By using the two shorter corridors the USAF would be able to get a higher rate of utilisation. The tonnage that required a C–54 to take one and a half hours from Rhein-Main required only an hour from the RAF bases located at Fassberg and Celle-Wietzenruch.

The expansion needed at Fassberg to meet airlift standard involved a huge programme of works services, RAF airfield construction teams, the clearance of some five acres (two hectares) of forest, and the laying of about 180,000 square yards (150,498m²) of PSP hardstanding and five miles (8km) of railway sidings. It was initially for use by RAF Dakotas, and the huge hardstandings – 800yd by 500yd (731m by 457m) – were ready for use in just seven days. Fassberg was handed over to the USAF on 22 August 1948 when forty C–54 Skymasters from the 50th Troop Carrier Wing

Above: World War Two pierced steel planking (PSP) for a new runway needed at Tempelhof is seen being unloaded from a USAF C–47 Skytrain transport. It was 7 July 1948 when the first twenty Douglas C–54 Skymasters to carry coal into Berlin landed at Tempelhof. By 15 July the US effort numbered fifty-four C–54 Skymasters and 104 C–47 Skytrains operating into the city. (A–67610A USAF)

moved in. The base was put under the command of Colonel Jack Coulter USAF along with his film star wife, Constance Bennett, who was often seen along with other wives serving coffee and doughnuts on the busy flight line.

The second airlift base in the British zone to be handed over to the USAF was Celle, and in mid-September 1948 the RAF Airfield Construction Wing units began converting the ex-Luftwaffe training station into a front-line airlift base. Approximately 2,000 German workers were employed on the extensive building programme. The huge task of building up Celle to meet airlift requirements involved the construction of a 5,400ft by 150ft (1,646m by 46m) runway, a PSP loading apron covering 190,000 square feet (17,651m²) and a 9,500ft by 50ft (2,895m by 15m) PSP taxiway. Other constructions included houses, rail facilities and a fuel storage complex. Celle was considered a model base for airlift needs. By mid-December it was ready to play its part as a CALTF despatching base. This enabled the 317th Troop Carrier Wing with its C–54 Skymasters to move in from Wiesbaden. On 16 December the first C–54 left for beleaguered Berlin, carrying food and coal. The 317th Troop Carrier Wing flew its 288th and last sortie on 31 July 1949.

Located near the beautiful old Hanseatic port of St Hubertus, full of tremendous character and antiquity, was the airfield at Lübeck built in 1935 for the Luftwaffe. After World War Two it became the Armament Practice Camp for RAF fighter squadrons. Many of the former Luftwaffe airfields were equipped with a railhead. Work required to bring the base up to airlift standard was extensive, involving an extension to the existing concrete runway, the laying of PSP hardstands and an 88,000 square yard (73,576m²) parking apron. The railhead capacity was doubled. Other major work services included the laying of a concrete road to the petrol bulk installation – about 4,000 square yards (3,344m²) in area – horizontal bar and centreline approach lighting and high-intensity runway lighting, plus lighting for the huge loading and unloading areas. The eastern boundary of Lübeck lay only two miles (3.2km) from the edge of the Russian zone and an instrument approach from that direction involved flying over Russian

territory. Lübeck was the main RAF Dakota base, the transports moving in from Fassberg on 22 August 1948 to be joined by civil Dakotas.

Originally Wunstorf was not a large airfield; it was constructed in 1934 as part of the huge Nazi expansion scheme. After World War Two it was occupied by a RAF fighter bomber Wing which remained until the airlift commenced. In July 1948 the air base had two concrete runways, perimeter tracks and hardstandings. The initially inadequate airfield became the base for both RAF Dakotas and Avro York transports. Heavy rain and the constant movement of aircraft and vehicles caused problems until the versatile PSP was brought in for the parking area. Eventually Wunstorf became the base for Avro Tudors, Lancastrians and Yorks.

On 5 October 1948 all eighteen civilian-operated Dakotas were moved out of Lübeck to Fuhlsbüttel, the civil airport for Hamburg, which was under the control of the Civil Aviation Commission of Germany. Now a designated airlift base, a new 5,850ft (1,783m) concrete runway was constructed parallel to the existing 4,800ft (1,463m) PSP strip, the new runway being ready for use by 21 December. A large well-illuminated tarmac loading apron was built and new airfield lighting installed. The lack of GCA at Fuhlsbüttel

Below: The feasibility of further expanding Tempelhof and Gatow was limited. A tract of land in the Tegel area of the French Zone was selected as a new air base. The US agreed to construct and operate it, with the French providing manpower to unload aircraft. Work commenced on 5 August 1948 with a target of completion of 1 January 1949. Berliners of all ages assisted the US Army engineers and the first USAF C–54 Skymaster landed on the new 5,500ft (1,676m) runway on 5 November. It became fully operational on 15 December and the first RAF aircraft to land at Tegel was Dakota KN446 on 18 November piloted by Sq/Ldr A.M. Johnstone of No.30 Squadron. (*R2028 MoD AHB*)

was a serious drawback.

Schleswigland was located on the Baltic coast and its base opened for airlift operation with the new RAF Hastings and the civilian-operated Halton transports on 25 November 1948. It was a large airfield with two excellent runways, but being on the coast it did suffer from low stratus, sea mist and low temperatures in the winter, and the location was the most distant from Berlin involving longer flying times.

The airlift was augmented on 5 July 1948 with the introduction of ten Short Sunderland flying boats from RAF Calshot, and these were based at Finkenwerder on the River Elbe west of Hamburg on the old site of the Blohm & Voss seaplane works. These aircraft airlifted supplies to Lake Havel adjoining Gatow airfield. The base at Finkenwerder was closed on 15 December due to the threat of ice forming on the Havelsee. The Americans showed great interest in the British flying boat operations and at one time there was talk of introducing the huge Martin JRM–1 Mars into airlift service.

As the airlift continued the need for an additional air base in Berlin became apparent, the feasibility of further expanding Tempelhof and Gatow being very limited. A search for a suitable site led to a tract of land in the French sector of Berlin once used as a training ground for the German Wehrmacht. The French were consulted and it was agreed the US would construct and operate the new base while the French would maintain it and provide manpower to unload

aircraft. Construction began on 5 August 1948 with a target completion date of 1 January 1949. A single runway 5,500ft by 150ft (1,676m by 46m) was built twenty-two inches (56cm) thick using tightly packed brick rubble and crushed rock taken from demolished buildings in the city. Large aprons totalling 120,000 square feet (11,148m²) and taxiways 6,020ft (1,835m) long, varying from 50ft to 120ft (15m to 36m) wide, were constructed. Access roads of 3,200ft by 40ft and 1,200ft by 20ft (975m by 12m and 366m by 6m) were constructed together with railroads totalling 2,750ft (838m). Buildings included operations, control tower, fire station, hospital, a warehouse, small hangar and many other vital facilities. On 15 December the new base was formally opened and the first aircraft to land was RAF Dakota KN446 on 18 November bringing in supplies from Lübeck.

It can be revealed that General Bill Tunner, the very able and experienced commander of the Combined Air Lift Task Force (CALTF), was planning for the blockade to continue for possibly a decade. There was in 1949 the possibility of flying coal into Berlin directly from the Ruhr, so initial plans were put into action to use the airfield located at Düsseldorf-Lohausen if required. Work commenced which furnished the airfield with a new instrument runway and a new high-intensity lighting system. However, by the time of completion the airlift had ended.

Below: In mid-September 1948 the RAF commenced converting Celle into an airlift base, employing some 2,000 German workers in the formidable task of constructing a 6,000ft (1,829m) runway, seen in this photo. A PSP loading apron covering 190,000 sq ft (17,651m²) and a PSP taxiway 9,500ft (2,896m) long were included. It was a perfect model for airlift needs with houses, rail facilities and a fuel storage complex. It was opened on 15 December 1948 as an operational base for four squadrons of USAF C–54 Skymasters. (*R2031 MoD AHB*)

Top: Busy scene at the new airfield at Tegel in the French sector with veteran steamrollers, some of pre-World War One vintage, packing down bricks collected from the ruins of Berlin. The specification was for a concrete runway two feet (609mm) thick, but as concrete was not available bricks were substituted. Work commenced in September and the new airlift airfield was ready in November and operational the following month. (*Landesbildstelle - Berlin*)

Above: The original control point for the RAF Short Sunderland operations was at Klara Lake on the US side of Havel Lake, but it was soon moved to the British side into the RAF yacht club which became Gatow Marine Base and was christened 'HMAFV Deadalus'. Shown here is a Sunderland flying boat from No.201 Squadron. (*Landesbildstelle - Berlin*)

Above: Each Sunderland carried four and a half tons of supplies into Berlin and brought out manufactured goods and undernourished refugees on each trip. Using DUKW amphibious vehicles and barges for unloading, the normal turn-around times were twenty minutes at Hamburg on the River Elbe, and twelve minutes at Havel Lake. In spite of fog and danger from floating debris, the flying boats made over 1,000 sorties, carried in 4,500 tons (4,572 tonnes) of food including vital salt, and flew out 1,113 children. (*Landesbildstelle - Berlin*)

Below: Scene at Tegel as the new airfield in the French sector progresses. Heavy equipment such as the huge caterpillar crane had to be flown in. It was cut up, flown in pieces, then welded together again. It was flown in the C–74 Globemaster or the C–82 Packet, or even a British Bristol 170 Freighter. German civilians – men, women and children – worked eight-hour shifts around the clock helping to carry rubble required for the new airfield. (*Landesbildstelle - Berlin*)

Men and Machines

The airlift had huge personal repercussions in the UK forces organisation, involving among others some 2,400 RAF National Service personnel due for release in September 1948 after completion of eighteen months' service. These included cooks, drivers, mechanical transport specialists, equipment personnel, radar fitters, wireless operators and even general duties clerks. Many were retained for the duration of the airlift.

Fortunately both Tempelhof and Gatow airfields had sufficient buildings and hangars to accommodate both airlift freight and the equipment needed for support services. In addition both had a civil airline operating in and out with daily scheduled services – BEA flew into Gatow and American Overseas Airlines into Tempelhof. In July 1948 at Gatow there were 513 RAF movements and 155 BEA. The station commander, Group Captain Brian Yarde, divided the station into two – operational and administrative – with Forward and Rear HQ respectively. The Air Traffic Control centre was Forward Operational HQ working twenty-four hours a day on an eight-hour shift system, each of the personnel completing on successive days a morning, an afternoon and a night shift followed by a day off. All units not directly concerned with the airlift became the Rear Administrative HQ where normal work hours were kept. The number of personnel, both service and civilian, increased dramatically in the first few weeks of the airlift. Prior to the blockade the total British ration strength was 580, a number which increased to 1,019 by 31 July and then to 3,500. The transit mess was serving 830 meals a day as against 220

Below: The capacious fuselage of the Globemaster I could accommodate either 125 troops, 115 stretchers and medical attendants, or up to 48,150lb (21,840kg) of cargo including ten Wright R–3350 radial engines, fifteen Allison V–1710 inline engines, two T–9EI light tanks, or two 105mm howitzers with tractors, ammunition and troops. Loading and unloading operations were facilitated by two onboard travelling cranes with a capacity of 8,000lb (3,629kg) and by the installation of a cargo lift. The size of the C–74 is emphasised by personnel looking at 42–65414 parked at Gatow, Berlin, during the airlift in 1948. (*Landesbildstelle – Berlin*)

Above: Royal Air Force Avro York transports being loaded with boxes containing cooking fat from British Army trucks at their base at Wunstorf during September 1948. It was 3 July 1948 when the first RAF Yorks commenced flying sorties to Berlin (Gatow). It was 29 August 1949 when the Yorks ceased to operate on the airlift, and Wunstorf ceased to operate as a 'Plainfare' station. (*R1786 MoD AHB*)

earlier. No extra cooking facilities were available. It was too much to hope that the many civilians working on the airlift would not be tempted by the large amounts of food they were handling daily, so it was necessary to have 120 military police and sixty watchmen for security purposes.

There were ten hangars at Gatow. All foodstuffs flown in, normally in York aircraft, were unloaded outside No.4 hangar. British supplies went to No.5 hangar on British Army trucks belonging to the Forward Airfield Supply Organisation (FASO), while German supplies went to No.6 hangar to be loaded onto German trucks for Berlin where it was handed over to the Magistrat. The hardstanding outside No.4 took a pounding and was constantly undergoing repairs, and it had to be extended for use as an aircraft dispersal area in bad weather. Coal was unloaded at No.10 hangar (a garage for FASO trucks), nicknamed 'Newcastle', then carried by rail to Kladow where a large ramp had been built beside the Havel Lake. This enabled coal to be tipped directly into barges, which was then transported to Berlin. It was possible to load two barges at once using this method. Of the remaining hangars No.1 was used for York overhauls; No.2 was occupied by No.5357 Airfield Construction Wing with some of its equipment; No.3 was the passenger hangar for BEA and RAF personnel; No.4 was the store for British and German freight and mail for back loading; No.7 was used for the vehicles of No.5357 Wing; No.8 was a garage for station and RAF Regiment vehicles; and No.9 was a store for civilian contractors working for No.5357 Wing.

There were many unique aspects to the airlift and a quick look at the British civilian and service participation reveals that many outposts and personnel, some of whom never saw Germany, were involved in the huge background organisation necessary to administer the humanitarian operation twenty-four hours a day. We shall never know the actual number involved.

It is not generally known outside airlift circles that a number of NCOs of the Glider Pilot Regiment acted as second pilots on RAF York and Hastings transports. Commencing in January 1949 the logbooks of these glider pilots began to show a considerable increase in monthly flying hour totals – one flew 100 hours in just over a month on the airlift. A total of fifteen NCO glider pilots came under the command of Captain Peter A. Downard, himself an airborne forces veteran, at Wunstorf, but

Below: Lieutenant Donald W. Measley USAF of Hammonton, New Jersey, based with the 54th Troop Carrier Sqadron, who completed forty supply missions to Berlin in a CALTF C–54 Skymaster is presented with a bouquet of flowers by nine-year-old Suzanna Joks of Berlin on the apron at Tempelhof. (*67616 AC USAF Douglas*)

Above Left: F/Lt Geoff Boston, Hastings pilot.

Above Right: 'Cass' Casselman, Hastings pilot, a Canadian.

not all were simultaneously engaged on flying duties. Half were based at Gatow as air movements specialists supervising the correct loading of aircraft flying back to their bases in the Western zone. Mail and goods manufactured in Berlin plus passengers were involved and the NCOs were trained to ensure the centre of gravity (C of G) was just where the pilot wanted it.

One of the NCOs, Roy Hanson, was detached from the Glider Pilot Regiment in December 1948 and attended an RAF quartermasters course at RAF Credenhill near Hereford. Roy was employed on flying duties as second pilot until March 1949 when he was transferred to Gatow to supervise the back loading of airlift transports until October 1949. Many, if not most, were veterans of airborne operations during World War Two. At Schleswigland the RAF Hastings base comprised a smaller group of NCO glider pilots under Captain P. Scott, an Arnhem veteran.

On 16 July 1949 Hastings TG611 crashed on take-off from Tegel during the early morning and the crew of five were killed including the co-pilot 7597167 Sgt Joe Toal of the Glider Pilot Regiment. Examination of the wreckage revealed that the cause of the accident was the incorrect setting of the elevator trimming tabs for take-off. They were set to the full nose-up position.

The first US Navy pilot to fly into Berlin was not on a 'Vittles' flight but on a 'Plainfare' flight with the British operation. On 7 October 1948 Lt A.M. Sindau was attached to one of the RAF Sunderland squadrons based at Finkenwerder near Hamburg.

The first US Navy R5D– Skymaster to arrive at Rhein-Main was from VR–8 Squadron piloted by Lt Richard Gerszeuski on 9 November 1948 followed by an R5D– from VR–6 Squadron piloted by Lt-Cdr David H. Minton the following day. This aircraft, piloted by Lt Joseph L. Norris and Lt (jg) Wayne L. Brooks, made a round trip to Tempelhof on 12 November. Despite the Soviets officially lifting the land blockade on 12 May 1949 both VR–6 and VR–8 squadrons continued to operate with the remainder of the 'Vittles' force.

The 5,000th airlift flight by VR–6 was a combined US Navy and US Air Force operation. Flying R5D– BuNo.56526 Lt (jg) Wayne L. Brooks, pilot, had 2/Lt W.V. Shumski of the USAF as co-pilot and AD3 Piermo P. Lucarelli as flight mechanic. The transport arrived home at Rhein-Main after the historic trip at 0627 hrs on 18 May.

On 12 January 1949 Cdr Harry P. Badger USN relieved Cdr Charles W. Howerton USN of command of Air Transport Squadron Six (VR–6).

The first two weeks of January 1949 were crucial. Food stores were adequate with a thirty-one day supply, but the coal stocks were dwindling at an alarming rate. It was forecast that within a week, or at the most ten days, stocks would be exhausted. Then Berlin would really suffer. The Allied authorities put into effect the most stringent energy cuts of the blockade. Despite the thermometer showing ten degrees below zero, gas and electricity supplies were reduced to a new low. The commandants took a further step to reduce Berlin's burden. More than 50,000 adults and 17,000 children were flown out to the Western zone by the RAF.

One of those involved in airlifting children out

Below: Hastings C1 TG564 with crew belonging to No.297 Squadron seen at Schleswigland in July 1949 during airlift operations. Left to right: Mike Hocking (flight engineer), Paddy Hutchinson (radio operator), Peter Innes (navigator), 'Cass' Casselman (pilot) and Geoff Boston (pilot). The crew completed 100 sorties. After conversion to the Hastings at Dishforth, Yorkshire, the squadron moved to Germany in December 1948 for airlift duty delivering coal to Berlin. On return flights, in addition to empty sacks, the Hastings brought back manufactured goods from Berlin factories.
(*F/Lt Geoff Boston*).

of Gatow was Ray Corbett, a Dakota pilot with No.77 Squadron who was aircrew on the second Dakota to operate on the airlift into Gatow in June 1948. Ray has described his experience with children.

'I made several such trips and they always caused me more concern than the usual ones. An aeroplane full of young children, some carried on in the arms of older ones, unable to understand English, often at night, seemed to me to carry far more responsibility than the more typical cargoes.

'When we picked them up at Gatow they would be loaded some 25 or 30 at a time by their German escorts harangued with a briefing in German, and the doors slammed shut. From then on they were all ours and some were very young. No interpreter to help out should an emergency situation arise. Can you blame me for being at least a little more concerned than usual?

'To occupy them on the day trips we often let them come up front in bunches of three or four at a time to have a look around. My faithful crew occasionally came up with a bright idea and one of them was to connect the windscreen de-icing tubes to a pair of gloves and attach them to the control column. When the blower was switched on it inflated the gloves and with the movements of the autopilot gave a very realistic impression of a robot in control of the aeroplane. You should have seen the expressions on the faces of our passengers when they saw this.

'The real problem arose after landing at Fassberg. A truck was supposed to meet each aeroplane that was carrying children and transport the load to a nearby transit centre. We often had to wait over an hour in a dispersal area at night with aircraft taxying around until a truck arrived. Safeguarding the children was rather like shepherding a flock of geese in the dark and not what we had signed on for at all. This led to some pretty hot R/T exchanges with the tower e.g. "Where's the bloody truck etc etc."

'However all's well that ends well and I did not hear of any unfortunate happenings and I suppose that the effort was made to reduce the rationing load in Berlin.'

Lt (jg) Leo M. 'Smokey' Sabota of VR–6 became the first US Navy pilot to complete 100 round trips to Tempelhof on 4 March 1949. Close behind was Lt (jg) Phillip R. Simmons who flew his 100th mission on 13 March. Third was Lt Herbert E. Bailey who completed his 100th mission on 15 March.

On 10 March Lt (jg) Wayne L. Brooks (pilot), Lt (jg) Loren L. Florey (co-pilot) and AD3 Bernard N. Carlock (flight mechanic) were practically stampeded by the unloading crew at Tempelhof as they disembarked from their VR–6 Skymaster for a snack at the chow wagon. Suspecting something unusual, Brooks asked what the reason was for so much hustle. He was told the unloading crew was attempting to establish a new unloading record, and this they did by unloading the transport in six minutes. Just twenty-seven minutes elapsed between landing and take-off, and this was also close to a record despite the fact that the VR–6 Skymaster had to wait its turn at the end of the runway.

Between the first and fifteenth of June 1949 VR–6 Squadron detached eighteen of its most venerable pilots. Collectively they had completed 2,547 flights on the airlift since arriving at Rhein-Main during November 1948.

In mid-1948 a high level meeting was held at the British Air Forces of Occupation (BAFO) HQ at Bad Eilsen under the chairmanship of Air Commodore Hatcher and attended by signals officers from both the RAF and the Royal Corps of Signals. The Berlin airlift was in its early stages and concern was now being expressed about the long-term reliability and availability of the land line communication between units in BAFO and the Allied enclave in Berlin. The land lines to Berlin from the west were routed through Magdeburg in the Russian-controlled east and were vulnerable to disruption. An independent and reliable alternative was urgently required, and the only one tried so far was a high-speed automatic Morse system operated from mobile vehicles of the Royal Corps of Signals. This was sited at the frontier post at Helmstedt, in full view of the Russian side of the control post. The type and role of the vehicles had been quickly identified by the Russians who soon set up

Below: Freight, possibly mail, from a RAF Avro York being hurriedly unloaded as a British Army truck waits to disperse its load of supplies to be airlifted to Berlin at Wunstorf. It is estimated that nearly forty Yorks were employed by the RAF on the airlift. The aircraft was often referred to by the Yanks as a four-fan, three-fin, Gooney Bird. Being high-wing, the 14,000lb (6,350kg) cargo load could be handled with ease. (*AP Photo Library*)

jamming counter-measures. It was now apparent that a more covert operation was needed to span the sixty miles dividing the Allied Forces in the west and the Berlin garrison in the east.

Operation 'Racehorse' developed during early 1944, and involved a radio telephone and telegraphy system capable of acting as a relay link within a land line network. It operated on a frequency of 28–30 MHz normally used in blind landing systems, but unusual as a communications frequency. The radio system together with two clever boxes from the GPO, a 1+4 and an S+DX, enabled simultaneous transmissions to be made on telephone and teleprinter over a distance of some eighty miles. The equipment was originally designed to provide both telephone and teleprinter communication from the bridgehead in Normandy to Operation 'Racehorse' units located on Beachy Head, thence via GPO lines to the huge control room at Uxbridge, Middlesex. Three units – Nos. 5183, 5184 and 5185 MSUs – were formed and operated until the end of hostilities. In late 1945 they, together with a mass of other vehicles, were placed in storage at Stade, a disused airfield north of Hamburg.

The 'Racehorse' system was well proven, reliable and mobile, but required a lot of space to set up. There were two large rhomboid aerial arrays, the diamond shape of which was some 200ft along its main line of shoot. For ideal operation the transmitting and receiving vehicles were some 200yds apart to eliminate interference. The power was supplied by a 15kv diesel generator. Working closely with the Royal Corps of Signals, two 'Racehorse' units were recovered from storage at Stade and modified to provide four telephone channels. Flying Officer Jack Clark together with an officer from the Signals, undertook a reconnaissance of the border area at Helmstedt in which two large aerial arrays were to be set up without attracting too much attention from the Russians. Two areas within the heavily wooded terrain were selected, and after some judicious tree felling the aerials were set up with the tops of the 70ft camouflaged masts just clearing the treetops. The specialist transmitting, receiving and power vehicles were sited and successful two-way tests carried out with other 'Racehorse' units operating in the Western zone.

Apparently it took an interesting display of international diplomacy to get the convoy of five vehicles, all bearing the markings of the Royal Corps of Signals but under RAF command, through the Russian control post at Helmstedt and onto the road into Berlin, from where 'Racehorse' operated successfully throughout the humanitarian operation.

Above: All cargoes airlifted into Berlin were valuable including the boxes of American manufactured cigars, seen here being loaded complete with checker and a military escort, aboard a RAF Dakota aircraft at Lübeck. The list of items carried on the airlift into the city was endless.
((A)363/3 AP Photo Library)

Above: RAF Dakota KN495 is shown at RAF Fassberg with German labourers loading sacks of coal. The transport was one of a large pool of RAF aircraft, many of the Dakotas originating from RAF Oakington, Cambridgeshire, early in 1948. Most were allocated an airlift identification number on the tail, which assisted in loading and unloading cargo for Berlin. Any squadron or unit identity the aircraft had was lost during the humanitarian airlift. (*R1762 MoD AHB*)

Below: Daily scene at Lübeck with passengers from Berlin and their belongings being loaded onto a British Army truck. The RAF Dakota in the background is KN446 still carrying the code 'PU' used by No.187 Squadron. It also carries the airlift number '70' used for loading and unloading identification. Delivered to the RAF in March 1945, KN446 was finally scrapped in February 1956.
(*Major Dave Becker, SAAF Museum*).

Above: Scene in the Ops Room at Rhein-Main air base with Captain Louis W. Baker (centre) receiving a block clearance from the duty Ops Officer before acting as 'block leader' of forty-seven Douglas C–54 Skymasters on a midnight flight to Berlin. The major problem of traffic flow along the narrow corridors to and from Berlin was solved by this 'time block' system, with each day and night divided into six cycles of four hours. Airlift bases were allotted a block of the precise times that the aircraft were required to reach the Fronau Eureka beacon sixteen miles from Berlin. (*67842 AC USAF Douglas*)

Left: The most celebrated pilot of the airlift was possibly Lt Gail S. Halvorsen USAF, known as 'the Chocolate Flyer', who introduced a unique candy drop to Berlin children gathered around the perimeter fence at the end of the landing runway at Tempelhof. Candy, chocolate and gum were tied up in parachutes made from handkerchiefs, old shirts and GI sheets etc. and dropped from the flare-chute in the C-54 on final approach. Halvorsen's bunk at Rhein-Main became a factory for miniature parachutes. (*Landesbildstelle - Berlin*)

Above: In 1948 as the Soviet strategy became clearer, plans were made by the Allies to enable the airlift to be maintained indefinitely. As more sorties were flown, all involved became more efficient. This included more effective utilisation on the ground. With the huge fleet of USAF C–54 Skymasters refuelling was cut from thirty-three to eight minutes, while the length of time required by twelve men to unload ten tons of bagged coal by hand at Tempelhof was reduced from seventeen to five minutes. Aircrews were forbidden to leave the flight line after landing. Flight information, weather briefing etc. were delivered to the aircraft on the tarmac. A mobile Post Exchange provided light meals and drinks, as seen in this photo taken at Tempelhof. (*AC 67953 USAF Douglas*)

Below: British South American Airways (BSAA) operated two Avro 688 Tudor I aircraft in its fleet. Registered G–AGRH and G–AGRJ, each was capable of airlifting 20,600lb (9,344kg) freight loads and they completed 114 and 117 sorties into Berlin. The other Tudors operated by BSAA were tankers. Shown here in the doorway of a Tudor I with Captain B.E. Patrick, who is on the right at the front, are Radio Officer Glyn Lloyd, First Officer Jan Gaynor, Signals Officer Roy Day, and an unknown at the top of the group. (*Roy Day*)

Below: Not usually mentioned is the huge exodus of passengers in and out of Berlin during the airlift, and the RAF retained a number of Dakotas fitted out for this task. The very young and elderly were flown out of Gatow, as seen in this photo showing the arrival at Lübeck. Official figures show the USAF flew 25,263 into Berlin and 37,486 out, while the RAF flew 34,815 in and 130,091 passengers out. (*A0363/6 AP Photo Library*)

Above: Winter scene at Tempelhof with the ramp and parking apron full of USAF and US Navy Skymasters. Centre of the photo is BuNo.87754 R5D–3 from VR–8 Squadron commanded by Commander James O. Voseller USN. The last 'Vittles' flight by the squadron was made on 31 July 1949. During the blockade the twenty-four Skymasters of VR–6 and VR–8 had logged 215,990 flight hours and carried 129,989 tons (132,068 tonnes) of supplies. (*Landesbildstelle - Berlin*)

Above Left: Airlift VIPs seen walking the apron during a visit to Tempelhof. These include, from the left: General Lucius Clay, US Military Governor of Berlin; Mr Ernest Bevin, British Foreign Secretary; General William H. Tunner, CALTF commander. Just behind is a friend of the author – Captain Raymond L. Towne, who served for many years with Bill Tunner as his personal assistant. Date of visit was 7 May 1949. (*Landesbildstelle - Berlin*)

Above Right: Douglas Dakota squadrons of the RAF Transport Command moved into Fassberg from overcrowded Wunstorf on 29 July 1948, remaining there until 22 August when Fassberg was handed over to the USAF for C–54 Skymaster operations. The Dakotas moved to Lübeck. Shown at Fassberg is a RAF Dakota being loaded with freight for Berlin. A second Dakota is in the background, and in the large hangar can be seen the rear end of a USAF C–54 Skymaster.
(*AP Photo Library*)

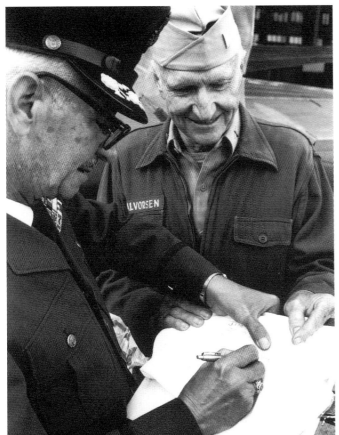

Left: At Tempelhof on the fortieth anniversary of the ending of the airlift, Gail Halvorsen the 'candy pilot', meets up with veteran James Spatafora who signs a handkerchief. (*US Air Force*)

Top: Crew of a British South American Airways Avro 688 Tudor at Wunstorf on 20 November 1948 headed by Captain W.H. Minns. The airline completed 261 sorties to Berlin with G–AGRG, G–AGRH, G–AGRJ stripped as Tudor Freighters or tankers. These aircraft were relatively new and so had low hours on the airframes and Merlin engines. (*Roy Day*)

Above Left: Mr Arthur Henderson, the Secretary of State for Air in the UK Labour government of the day, is seen talking to Nav2 Warwick Harper, a navigator with No.46 Squadron Dakotas, in the Operations Room at Lübeck during a visit to the busy airlift base. The squadron's home base was Oakington, Cambridgeshire, but during the airlift it was detached to Wunstorf, Fassberg, and finally Lübeck. The tour of airlift bases commenced on 14 May 1948. (*R2004 MoD AHB*)

Above Right: The Station Commander at RAF Lübeck, Group Captain A.J. Biggar, known as 'Wally', greets passengers flown in from RAF Gatow, Berlin, in Dakota KN657. Early in the airlift Wally was responsible for overseeing the construction work that was to turn RAF Fassberg into an operational 'Plainfare' base. This included the arrival of the USAF with Douglas C–54 Skymasters on 20 August 1948. The Dakota KN657 ex-No.53 Squadron joined RAF Transport Command at RAF Waterbeach on 10 March 1948, remaining on airlift duties until joining No.30 Squadron in 1949. (*AP Photo Library*)

Above Left: The unique air bridge to Berlin attracted many visitors from Allied nations. Mr Arthur Henderson is seen talking to F/Sgt Norman Healey and F/Sgt Charles Cole, both Air Quartermasters on Dakotas. The status board behind the group lists the serials and airlift identification numbers of nearly thirty RAF Dakotas. (*R2008 MoD AHB*)

Left: The 317th Troop Carrier Wing (Heavy) with its squadrons – 39th, 40th, 41st and 46th – with C–54 Skymasters moved into RAF Celle from Wiesbaden on 16 December 1948. The new rebuilt air base (APO 147) housed 443 officers and 2,799 enlisted ranks, American and British. Depicted is the late Doug Pirus near the flight line at Celle, a member of the American Aviation Historical Society (AAHS) and a friend of the author. Doug did some invaluable photography during the airlift. (*Doug Pirus*)

Air Traffic Control

Commencing June 1945 the Western powers had only verbal agreements from the Russians for rail and road access to Berlin. The necessity for air safety led to important written agreements concerning air traffic control by the Allied Control Council in November 1945 and October 1946. In November 1945, with Russian agreement, the Western powers proposed three twenty-mile-wide air corridors connecting Berlin with Hamburg, Frankfurt-Rhein-Main, and Hanover-Bückeburg. From this came a set of SOPs (Standard Operating Procedures) or flight rules published by the Allied Control Authority Air Directorate on 22 October 1946, these proving to be crucial.

The rules not only further defined the air corridors, but also led to the setting up of the Berlin Control Zone which permitted aircraft landing and taking off from Berlin airfields to fly within a twenty-mile (32km) radius of the city. This allowed Allied aircraft to overfly the Soviet sector of Berlin and the Soviet Zone on approach and departure. The agreement did not specify altitude but by practice and custom Allied aircraft adopted a 10,000ft ceiling.

In Kleist Park, about a mile from the famous 'bunker', stood a large neo-baroque building which had escaped the wartime Allied bombing holocaust. It was the former Russian Supreme Court and later the Nazi People's court, and in 1945 it became the headquarters of the Allied Control Authority, the four-power government for all Germany. The building emptied due to the Soviet withdrawal in 1948, except for one element. Here, the remaining vestige of four-power co-operation continued to function until German reunification in 1990 in the shape of the vital Berlin Air Safety Centre. Manned by officers and NCOs from the four wartime Allied air forces it was originally tasked with 'approving and regulating' the flights of all aircraft using the quadripartite Berlin airspace including the three very active air corridors in and out of the Western zones.

Guiding the aircraft in and out of the Gatow and Tempelhof, and later Tegel, airfields in Berlin at three-minute intervals in all weathers was one of the most difficult and stressful tasks of the entire airlift operation. Military air traffic controllers and communications specialists of the Allies, mainly the USAF and RAF, plus many civilian air specialists brought over from the USA to assist were involved. The huge US Airways Air and Airways Communication Service (AACS) supplied the radio navigation aids, manned the control towers, radio

Below: Daily scene at an airlift base, possibly RAF Lübeck, with RAF Dakotas and at least one USAF Skymaster parked, waiting to be loaded for the next flight down the corridor into Berlin. With the formation of CALTF its mechanism was capable of launching an airborne cargo every three minutes day and night. The photo depicts the RAF airman flashing a green light to the taxying RAF Dakota with the aid of an Aldis lamp.
(*R1774 MoD AHB*)

Above: By September 1948 the influx of USAF personnel to the airlift theatre on TDY (temporary duty) stood at 1,320 officers and 3,605 airmen, figures which rose to 2,374 officers and 7,563 airmen by the end of the year. Airlift Task Force HQ – later CALTF HQ – was based at Wiesbaden. Shown in Base Operations are Corporal Clyde J. Dhein, a native of Sheboygan, Wisconsin, on the left, with Major Harold H. Sims, Chief of Navigation & Briefing in the centre, and Captain Raymond L. Towne, Assistant Chief of Operations under General William Tunner, and a good friend of the author, on the right. (*67982 A.C. Douglas*).

---

ranges, radio beacons, the radar equipment and other air traffic control facilities.

On 11 December 1948 a block flight of RAF Dakotas was arriving at Gatow when a similar block of Douglas C–54 Skymasters was diverted from Tempelhof because of a crash blocking the runway. The C–54s were fitted in between the Dakotas so that between 1300 and 1400 hrs thirty-seven aircraft landed and seventeen took off. In the next hour twenty-one landed and thirty-seven took off, making a total of 112 movements in two hours – nearly one per minute. Before the end of December a further 2,031 landings were made at Gatow, the total sorties during the month being 6,737. The airlift had been operating 187 days with an average of 278 landings per twenty-four hours, or one every five minutes or so day and night for six months, making Gatow the busiest airfield in the world, having handled 321,620 short tons of freight, one ton every fifty-three seconds. The GCA (Ground Controlled Approach) radar had completed 3,654 talkdowns with only 2.6 per cent overshoots when the aircraft had to abandon the approach and either position for another landing attempt, which was rare, or, as was often the case, return to its base.

At this time one of the runways at Gatow was still PSP (pierced steel planking) and it was receiving a hammering by the high impact of loaded aircraft, and was serviced if possible during the lulls between blocks of aircraft arriving. The

5357 Airfield Construction Wing based at Gatow, which included Squadron Leader Lew J.B. Cass and Flight Sergeant Groves, would inspect the runway and mark serious defects with a red flag, and less serious ones with a yellow. A team of German civilians followed, dealing with the worst first and trying to complete the repairs before the next wave of aircraft.

Both the ATC and GCA controllers were soon suffering from fatigue and as there was a shortage of control officers in the RAF, the Royal Navy loaned two ATC and two GCA controllers for duties at Gatow. They were soon incorporated into the watch list.

From the early days of air traffic control, it was recognised that in conjunction with radio communication aids, an extension of the controllers' sight was required. This was essential if large volumes of aircraft were to be managed, especially in adverse weather conditions where the pilot could not provide adequate visual separation. The US government called in the Gilfillan Brothers of Los Angeles to assist in the development of a ground controlled approach radar. On 30 December 1943 the first GCA units rolled off the production line for field tests. The production models of the early AN/MPN–1 subsequently demonstrated the operational value of GCA. Production contracts went to Gilfillan, Bendix and the Federal Telephone and Radio Corporation. After World War Two came the CPN–4 and the

AN/MPN–11 models, with Gilfillan being the largest producer.

It was fortuitous that the RAF, the USAF and the US Navy operated the same GCA units and were able to equip most of the airlift airfields. It meant a twenty-four hour operation so technicians and controllers alike soon became proficient on the relatively new invention. The huge humanitarian operation was a crucial test for GCA radar. The records reveal that the RAF had No.5 GCA unit at Gatow in 1947 with No.4 GCA unit at Wunstorf. Tempelhof had a CPN–4 (XW) which was one of five development models for the production AN/CPN–4. It was only completed early in 1948 and was flown across the Atlantic in preparation for the airlift. On the first of April 1949 three US Navy GCA units were moved into Rhein-Main and reported to VR–6 Squadron for administrative purposes. GCA Unit 21 arrived from NAS Squantum, Massachusetts, Unit 28 from NAS Grosse Ille, Michigan, and Unit 31 from NAS Willow Grove, Pennsylvania. Six officers and thirty-four enlisted men were included.

All navigation on US airlift flights was done by the pilots using radio aids and information received from ground radar stations, while the RAF carried a navigator and often a signaller. Tempelhof was equipped with a CPS–5 search radar located on the airfield buildings, the control room being directly below the control tower. This had six twelve-inch (30.5cm) remote viewing scopes. While the CPS–5 was in operation there were no mid-air collisions and the radar undoubtedly contributed greatly to air safety in the crowded Berlin area. When as many as three aircraft appeared simultaneously at the seventy-mile (113km) outer range ring of the radar scope, operators controlled them into two-minute space separation before they reached the Tempelhof radio range. This separation, co-ordinated with the appropriate GCA unit, enabled a standard procedure landing and was an outstanding achievement by the approach control radar. The biggest accolade came from the pilots. The airlift bases were equipped with two GCA units and Flight Lieutenant W.C. Ager maintained records which reveal that between July 1948 and 28 August 1949, while GCA controller at RAF Wunstorf, he personally talked down 196 Yorks, sixty-one Tudors, fifty-two Lancastrians, forty-nine Dakotas, twenty Halifaxes, ten Haltons, three Hastings, one Viking, two Skymasters and a single C–45 Expeditor. This was in a cloudbase (QBB) as low as 100ft (30.5m) and visibility (QBA) down to seventy-five yards (69m).

Below: The busy Operations Room of the Berlin Air Safety Centre located in the Allied Control Commission building in the American sector of Berlin. Here the Allied air traffic controllers – American, British, French and Russian – using coloured flight progress strips, monitored and co-ordinated the flights from all four nations. (*Daily Mirror*)

As winter approached in 1948/49 strict weather minima were in force. Tempelhof landings were difficult due to the presence of five-storey apartment block buildings, so a four-degree glide path was imposed requiring a 750ft/min (229m/min) rate of descent. Visibility minima was one mile (1.6km). Wiesbaden and Rhein-Main minima was 300ft (91m) ceiling and half a mile (805m) visibility, while all other airlift bases were standard 200ft (61m) and half a mile (805m) visibility. During that winter the record achieved in movements into Berlin was an outstanding one. The GCA radar units played a key role in this, with landings at four- or five-minute intervals throughout the winter. From September 1948 to March 1949 at Tempelhof a total of 13,947 'IFR' (Instrument Flight Rules) approaches were made. Of these seventeen per cent were made below the minima, and only slightly above two per cent were missed approaches.

Each USAF GCA had its radio call-sign, these being listed in the Airlift Routes & Procedures CALTF Manual 60–1 as JIGSAW (Tempelhof), CORKSCREW (Tegel), SPIKEY (Wiesbaden), ROCKFISH (Rhein-Main), ZIGZAG (Fassberg), HOTPOINT (Celle), SKIPPER (Burtonwood).

Below: Air traffic control clerks from the US Air Force and the RAF plus the French Air Force handle signals in the Berlin Air Safety Centre. At the end of the desk in this 1948 photograph sits, in isolation, a Soviet air traffic controller, Senior Lieutenant Komarov, who apparently objected strongly to being photographed.
(*Daily Mirror*)

Radio call-signs for airlift aircraft varied, with the RAF mainly using the prefix 'RAFAIR' followed by the last three digits of the aircraft airframe number. 'RAFAIR 333' (York MW333) became known on the airways as 'State Express' after a well-known brand of US cigarettes. After unloading, the aircraft taxied to the end of the runway joining a long queue, and naturally in the waiting period some jocular language was passed between pilots and the control tower, an example being: 'From the man on the ground to the man in the tower, give me the word and I'll give it the power.'

After General Bill Tunner had sorted out the shambles for the early traffic flow system into Berlin, the new traffic control system made use of different altitudes in the corridors. A vertical separation of 500ft (152m) was utilised, this being sufficient to allow more aircraft to use the air corridors at the same time. Under the new system the southern corridor was used exclusively for traffic from Rhein-Main and Wiesbaden to Berlin; the northern corridor carried traffic from Celle, Fassberg, and all the RAF bases; while the central corridor was used by USAF traffic returning to their bases. These measures increased safety in the air considerably and satisfied Tunner.

Normally the airlift transports took off at intervals of at least three minutes and on a typical flight from Rhein-Main, aircraft climbed straight ahead to 900ft (274m) on the QNH which indicated the altimeter setting in inches above sea level. The RAF and civil aircraft altimeter was set in millibars. At altitude aircraft turned south and homed on to the Darmstadt Beacon crossing this at 3,000ft (914m). This took five minutes. From Darmstadt the pilot homed on to the

Below: Photo shows a typical ATC Operations Room during the airlift with RAF personnel monitoring frequencies, writing all the transmissions down in long-hand. There were no recording tape facilities available. The movement board shows a civil Halifax G–AIWP of Skyflight inbound from 'DAHF' Hamburg/Finkenwerder, and a Dakota '514' inbound from 'DABU', airfield identification unknown.
(*R1833 MoD AHB*)

Aschaffenburg Beacon, eight to ten minutes away, climbing to the assigned altitude of either 5,000 or 6,000ft (1,524 or 1,829m). On reaching the assigned altitude the airspeed was increased to 170 mph (273 km/h) which was maintained in the corridor. Once the Aschaffenburg Beacon was reached the pilot turned towards the Fulda Range station, this leg taking fifteen minutes. Navigation aids at Fulda included a low frequency range and a visual-aural radio range (VAR). When crossing Fulda the pilot relayed his time, altitude and in-flight conditions for the benefit of the stream ahead and behind him. Using the Fulda aids he was able to establish a definite compass heading to take him through the corridor.

Forty minutes after Fulda, or at the Kornorn intersection – an ILS range leg closing the corridor at a ninety-degree angle – the pilot called Tempelhof Airways, relaying a position report which enabled him to be picked up by the CPS–5 radar and to be given an identification turn. Depending on the weather the pilot was instructed to contact either Tempelhof tower or 'Jigsaw', which was the Tempelhof GCA. Two runways were in use at Tempelhof, one for landing and one for take-off. On landing the transport was met by a 'Follow Me' signed jeep which led the aircraft to a slot on the ramp. Then came the unloading, a meeting with a weather officer for a return flight brief, and most important of all the portable snack bar. Unloading was accomplished in twenty to thirty minutes by a German crew of a dozen.

Below: The crew of an RAF Avro York transport seen in the Ops Briefing Room prior to their flight. The first twelve Yorks arrived at RAF Wunstorf during the evening of 12 July 1948. By 20 July some forty of the type were involved airlifting their contribution to the then daily tonnage of 750 tons (762 tonnes). Both RAF and British registered civilian Yorks were eventually employed on the airlift, the military version soldiering on until August 1949.
(*R1800 MoD AHB*)

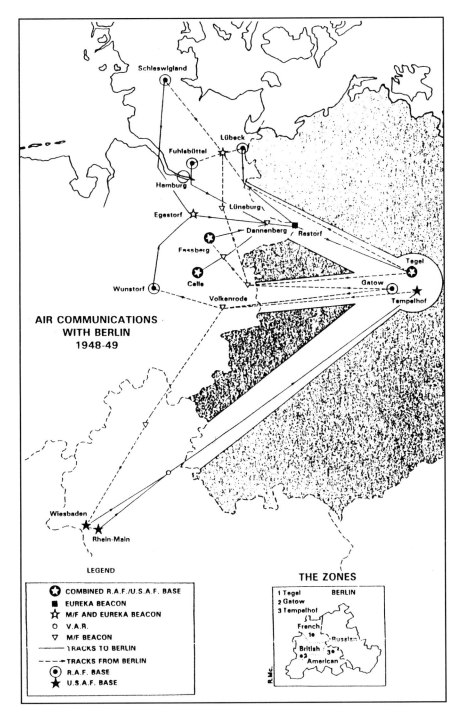

AIR COMMUNICATIONS
WITH BERLIN
1948-49

LEGEND

⊛ COMBINED R.A.F./U.S.A.F. BASE
■ EUREKA BEACON
☆ M/F AND EUREKA BEACON
○ V.A.R.
▽ M/F BEACON
——▸ TRACKS TO BERLIN
----▸ TRACKS FROM BERLIN
⊙ R.A.F. BASE
★ U.S.A.F. BASE

THE ZONES

BERLIN
1 Tegel
2 Gatow
3 Tempelhof
French 1●
British ●2 Russian
American 3●

Above: Flight safety was a high priority throughout the period of the airlift and there were no mid-air collisions. The radar at the airlift air bases and the many navigation aids in the corridors undoubtedly contributed greatly to air safety, especially in the heavily congested Berlin airspace. The successful spacing of traffic at set time intervals was sufficient to permit identification and pick-up by radar (CPS–5 at Berlin) before a hand-over to GCA for landing. It was an outstanding achievement and a credit to all the ATC operators and the technicians who maintained the equipment.

Fortunately for the Allies, the Russians had agreed to Berlin being served by three air corridors, subject to the restrictions of passage over the Soviet Zone imposed by the Quadripartite Agreement of November 1945. Each corridor was twenty statute miles (32km) wide, extending from ground level to 10,000ft (3,048m). Two terminated in the British Zone, leading to Hamburg and Hanover, and one in the American Zone, leading to Frankfurt. The Hamburg corridor crossed ninety-five miles (153km) of the Soviet Zone from Berlin to the nearest point of the British Zone; the Hanover corridor was 117 miles (188km) long and the Frankfurt corridor 216 miles (347km). No radio or radar navigation aids were available in Soviet-occupied territory. All three corridors terminated in the Berlin Control Zone, a circular area of twenty statute miles (32km) radius from 52°30′N, 13°22′E, centred on the Allied Control Council's building.
(*MoD AHB*)

Above: By 1948 the RAF had nine squadrons equipped with the Avro York, all of which participated on the airlift. This excellent transport, developed from the equally successful Lancaster bomber, made 29,000 flights to Berlin and carried approximately 239,000 tons (242,825 tonnes) of supplies. This was nearly half of the total contribution made by the RAF. In addition Skyways operated three civil-registered Yorks on the airlift. The photo shows an RAF York on final approach. (*Landesbildstelle - Berlin*)

Below: Landings at Tempelhof were more difficult than at any other airlift base due to the presence of huge five-storey apartment buildings around the perimeter and adjacent to the final approach. The GCA radar glide path was four degrees, requiring a descent of 750 ft/min (229 m/min). Even this brought incoming aircraft to within fewer than 100ft (30m) of the roofs of surrounding buildings. Three USAAF C–54 Skymaster aircraft were wrecked at Tempelhof due to landing too far down the runway, but no accidents were recorded through landing short. Shown here is a C–54 'coming down the slot' between buildings at Tempelhof. (*Douglas*)

Above: Vivid night shot taken at Wiesbaden during the round-the-clock airlift operation with C–47s and vehicles silhouetted while being loaded with vital supplies for Berlin. The blaze of light in the background is from the maintenance hangar, where USAF crews operated a streamline turn-around inspection system. The streaks of light in the right background are from transports converging on the take-off runway. Other streaks are from ground vehicles. (*67994 AC USAF Douglas*)

Left: The Royal Air Force assigned three GCA radar units to airlift bases in Germany with detachments as required; these were Nos.4, 5 and 11. Shown here are RAF technicians checking a Gilfillan MPN–1 GCA truck at an airlift base in Germany.
(*R1814 MoD AHB*)

Below: The Douglas C–54 Skymasters concentrated in Germany for the airlift came from bases in the USA, Alaska, Hawaii and the Caribbean. This photo shows a daily scene at Rhein-Main as the four-engined transports line up waiting for clearance to take off for the flight to Berlin with supplies.
(*67613 AC USAF Douglas*)

Above: Tempelhof had only one runway and prior to the airlift US Army engineers built a twelve-foot-thick rubble base runway covering it with PSP. Due to the continuous pounding of heavily loaded aircraft the metal surface started to break. It took over 200 maintenance personnel to keep it in service between landings. In early July 1948 a new runway was built, and later in the year a third runway was commenced. Photo shows a C-54 Skymaster on final approach to the PSP runway.
(*69184 AC USAF Douglas*)

Left: Two GCA units were installed at each of the airlift bases. At all bases except those in the Berlin area, which presented special problems, the two units were installed back to back on the same side of the runway and on the same hardstand. Fortunately all the GCA units used on the airlift originated at the Gilfillan stable, but came from locations far and wide. The US Navy airlifted three GCA units from three bases in the USA, while the RAF had No.4 GCA unit at Wunstorf and No.5 at Gatow in 1947. Shown are two GCA units at Celle which was a USAF C–54 base (*Doug Pirus*)

Below: By August 1945 the USAF had 839 Douglas C–54 Skymasters in service on a worldwide network of routes. The US Navy flew 192 Douglas R5D– Skymasters on domestic Pacific routes. A total of thirty-eight C–54E models were stripped for carrying coal on the airlift, re-designated C–54M. Shown here in the early morning mist at RAF Gatow are the early Skymaster arrivals from RAF Fassberg, waiting to be unloaded with their precious cargo of industrial coal. This C–54, 42–72559 c/n 10664 was delivered from the Douglas factory on 12 April 1945.
(*A–68696 AC Douglas*)

Left: CALTF agreed that the operation of the airlift to Berlin would have been seriously curtailed without the use of GCA radar, which was the primary let-down and landing aid at most of the air bases. Gilfillan were the manufacturers of the GCA units operated on the airlift, which included the MPN–1 and CPN–4. The USAF records from 1 June 1948 to 30 April 1949 show that out of 224,197 landings made at USAF bases, 52,736 were made by the use of GCA. It was operated and manned by US Airways & Air Communications Service (AACS) personnel. Photo shows a C–54 Skymaster taking off over the GCA unit at Tempelhof, Berlin.
(*USAF Douglas*)

Below: The night scene at Tempelhof is a pattern of lights as USAAF C–54 Skymasters are being unloaded. Seventeen minutes after landing in Berlin, the transports take off on the return shuttle flight to bases located at Wiesbaden, Rhein-Main or Fassberg. The C–54 on the right of the photo is 45–529 c/n 35982, delivered to the huge Military Air Transport Service (MATS) on 14 July 1945.
(*67609 AC Copy Neg B27–12–1 Douglas*)

Above: Engine fitters, including Corporal Margaret Fisher BEM from Poole, Dorset, work on a Pratt & Whitney R–1830–90 Twin Wasp starboard engine of an RAF Dakota operating on the airlift. With hangar space at a premium a lot of the servicing had to be carried out in the open, with the ground crews braving the weather elements. During the night of 2 July 1948, it rained so hard at RAF Wunstorf that no fewer than twenty-six RAF Dakotas parked outside were put out of service temporarily by electrical faults. (*R1843 MoD AHB*)

Maintenance and Overhaul

During the height of the airlift the US had 354 Douglas C–54 Skymasters allocated to the operation, with an average daily number of 128 available in commission, actually carrying supplies into Berlin. The remainder were involved in a maintenance programme or waiting for spare parts. The average Skymaster was flying eight to ten hours per day, not counting loading and unloading or time for crew changes etc.; each aircraft was making four to five trips a day to and from Berlin. However, on the Fassberg to Tegel route three trips were accomplished in an eight-hour flight period.

The C–54 had been employed as a passenger aircraft by the huge worldwide US Military Air Transport Service so it had to be modified for cargo hauling. It was carrying heavier loads than it was designed for, and making numerous take-offs and landings at glide-angles that caused hard landings. There was inevitably excessive ground idle time while transports waited in line for take-off clearance. All of these factors plus others, including the coal that was normally carried, caused abnormal maintenance problems. Ten tons of coal in the form of ligulate briquettes in 100lb (45.5kg) buslap bags were normally carried. During the usual twenty-minute turn-round back at Fassberg the oil in all four engines would be changed if due, and another ten tons of coal loaded. A friend of the author, Robert R. Lawrence, flew no fewer than 180 missions from Fassberg to Tegel.

The US Air Force required that fifty-hour maintenance checks be performed at the home air base in Germany, so work went on at these bases twenty-four hours a day, seven days a week. When the C–54 had completed three intermediate fifty-hour maintenance inspections and was nearing a fourth, a more technical check was necessary and initially the transports were flown to Oberpfaffenhofen depot in the US Zone near Munich which, with effect from 5 August 1948, had been converted as a huge maintenance depot for the purpose of performing 200-hour inspections on airlift aircraft. After four such 200-hr cycles the aircraft was flown back to the USA to contractor facilities located in New York, Texas or California for a complete 1,000-hr inspection known as IRAN (Inspection Repair As Necessary). This was the cycle for regular scheduled maintenance, not taking into account engine failures, accidents and other unscheduled field maintenance and repairs. It soon became apparent why it took 354 aircraft to keep an average of 128 C–54s in daily operation.

On the first day of September 1948 work commenced at the huge air depot located at Burtonwood, Lancashire, in order to replace Oberpfaffenhofen as the major US maintenance depot in Europe. On 12 September personnel from the 59th Air Depot began arriving by sea at Liverpool to reopen Burtonwood after two years back under RAF control. Shortly after they had settled down, not only were they undertaking 200-hr overhauls on airlift C–54s but also maintenance on Boeing B–29 Superfortress aircraft from three fully equipped bomb groups consisting of ninety aircraft based at four RAF airfields in the United Kingdom for what was officially described as 'routine training'. The overhaul programme was organised on a production line basis starting with the removal of all loose equipment for checking, followed by a complete clean internally and externally, before being passed on for engine and flight system checks. By February 1949 seven C–54s from the airlift were delivered in one twenty-four-hour period, this being increased in March to eleven delivered in one day, and a total of eighty-three C–54s in tip-top condition returned to Germany in the first fifteen days of March.

To ensure the transports were on the ground for the shortest possible period Burtonwood personnel worked a round-the-clock three-shift day. These aircraft had carried everything from coal and flour to razor blades and soap powder, and the inevitable spillage caused considerable problems for the cleaning crews. Most C–54s made several visits to Burtonwood between October 1948 and May 1949.

Transport Command had its major servicing unit located at RAF Honington, Suffolk, established on 28 February 1946 as a maintenance and modification unit. It was responsible in 1948/49 for ensuring that aircraft supplying the marooned city of Berlin with the vital necessities of life were never kept on the ground for lack of vital supplies. The unit itself operated six Dakota transports as 'Plumber Flight' which each month flew 60,000 miles (96,540km) and carried between 400 and 500 tons (406 and 508 tonnes) of spares, not only to airlift bases in Germany, but also to transport bases in the United Kingdom. All aircraft employed on the airlift had a much higher landing rate so the strain on tyres, brakes and undercarriages increased generally. In addition to Dakotas this included the Avro Yorks and the Handley Page Hastings transports. The latter type joined the airlift on 1 November 1948.

Honington served as a clearing house for all the individual spares required by airlift aircraft in Germany. Signals to this servicing unit were categorised as AOG – Aircraft On Ground – or IOR – Immediate Operational Requirements. These demands ensured immediate priority. On receipt of a demand, Honington relayed it to the appropriate RAF Maintenance Unit (MU) and the spares were flown out on the first available aircraft.

Dakotas returned to Oakington, Cambridgeshire for servicing were found to have accumulated a considerable layer of coal dust and flour under the flooring. To remove this was a task which required many man-hours. Preventive measures had to be found quickly and the difficulty was soon overcome with a touch of typical RAF ingenuity: joints in the floor were sealed with Plasticine, about 26lb being required to seal the floor of a Dakota. This treatment was completely effective.

Many civil aviation contractors were called upon not only to assist with the refurbishing of stored Dakotas in the MUs but also in the overhaul of those operating on the airlift. Scottish Aviation at Prestwick, Scotland, overhauled a total of seventy-one Dakotas between August 1948 and May 1949, all for the airlift. Similarly, Airwork Limited at Eastleigh, Southampton, undertook major servicing

on no fewer than eighty-nine airlift Dakotas between September 1948 and July 1949. Field Aircraft Services at Tollerton near Nottingham performed major overhauls, while their huge engine division located at Croydon airport, Surrey, maintained and repaired Pratt & Whitney R–1830–90 Twin Wasp engines for the Dakotas.

In Germany hangar accommodation was at a premium so many transports had to be parked outdoors, and this often caused problems. On the night of 2 July 1948 it rained so hard at Wunstorf that twenty-six Dakotas were temporarily put out of service with electrical faults. The lack of repair facilities at the Berlin airfields also became a problem. General Bill Tunner decided that any USAF aircraft which lost an engine on its way into Berlin would have to be flown out empty and on three engines back to its base. A three-engine take-off for a four-engined aircraft is an unpleasant undertaking and the difficult task was entrusted to instructor pilots who were very experienced. Apparently the C–54 took off very well empty on three engines.

By the beginning of October 1948 the MATS organisation had no further reserves of Skymasters to commit to the airlift, whose task force was still short of its requirements. Two US Navy R5D–Skymaster squadrons – VR–6 at Agana, Guam, and VR–8 at Hickam, Honolulu – were given orders to join the airlift at a few hours' notice. The transports were flown to Moffett Field near San Francisco where all the passenger-carrying aircraft were

Below: The C–54 Skymaster wash dock installation at the Oberpfaffenhofen air depot located near Munich, used in the first stages of 200-hour inspections for the transports engaged on the airlift. The base was more commonly known as 'Oberhuffin-puffin'. Three variants of the C–54 were used on the airlift, the Model C–54D, E and G.
(*Doug Pirus*)

Above: The Berlin airlift was the greatest air transport operation of all time, and keeping it in operation was a logistical headache. The RAF established 'Plumber Flight' based at RAF Honington, Suffolk, equipped with six Dakotas which each month flew over 60,000 miles (96,540km) and carried between 400 and 500 tons (406 and 508 tonnes) of spares, not only to the bases in Germany but to RAF Transport Command bases in the United Kingdom. The landing rate of all aircraft on the airlift was so high that the strain on tyres, brakes and undercarriages was severe. Shown in the hangar at Honington during November 1948 is 'Plumber Flight' Dakota KN564 parked behind a line of Merlin engines for Avro Yorks waiting to be airlifted. The Dakota joined 'Plumber Flight' on 27 September 1948 being transferred to No.240 Operational Conversion Unit at RAF Dishforth, Yorkshire, on 22 June 1949 to be employed in converting Dakota pilots for the airlift. (*Quadrant Picture Library*)

exchanged for R5D– freighters drawn from other units. At Jacksonville, Florida, the aircraft were fitted with extra radio and radar equipment with the first reaching Rhein-Main on 9 November. Each US Navy squadron had twelve aircraft with nine in service at any one time. Initially the Navy technicians were permitted to carry out all maintenance up to the 1,000-hr check on the squadron. However, the USAF insisted the R5Ds had to go to Burtonwood air depot for their 200-hr and subsequent checks. Maintenance support for US Navy airlift transports was provided in the USA by VR–1 at Patuxent River, Maryland, and heavy maintenance by VR–44 at Moffett Field, California. The last VR–6 transports to go to Burtonwood for overhaul were BuNo.56507 on 18 December 1948, 56492 on the 20th, and 50855 on the 24th. Hereafter all 200-hr checks were once more made at Rhein-Main and heavy maintenance at Moffett Field. The first R5D– to fly to the USA for heavy maintenance departed on 4 January 1949 piloted by Lt Robert C. Haggerton. Four R5D– aircraft were returned to the USA for heavy maintenance during the month of June 1949. BuNo.50852 flown by Lt Edgar B. Roper departed from Rhein-Main on the 13th. It was followed by 56524 piloted by Alan R. Funkey two days later. On the 22nd and 28th BuNo.56541 and 56492 left for Moffett's production overhaul line with Lt William C. Kerber and Ensign Bruce van Atta as pilots.

During April 1949 the engineering department of VR–6 initiated several organisational changes which paid substantial dividends. Special check crews who completed all checks during daylight hours were organised, and RB19–R2 platinum spark plugs were installed in all engines. As a result, the average time for 200-hr inspections was reduced from thirty-six to six to eight hours, and intermediate checks were cut from ten to six and a half or seven hours. These improvements paid off with more sorties flown per day per aircraft.

Support for the humanitarian airlift came from many quarters. On 1 August 1948 VR–3 Squadron cancelled all its worldwide commitments and from Patuxent River, Maryland, operated flight schedules with spares etc. to Germany with twelve round-trip transatlantic crossings per week. The first such flight was on 26 July 1948 piloted by Lt (jg) Mullin.

Naturally there was competition between the US Navy and the USAF with races against the clock involving unloading and maintenance. A major reason for the US Navy squadrons consistently breaking records was the more qualified maintenance personnel per aircraft. Many maintenance innovations were embraced and these, plus other preventive methods employed, were the greatest factors in setting the record of 130 days' flying for a total of 32,540 engine-operating hours without an engine failure.

Above: Personnel from the 59th Air Depot Wing at Burtonwood working on an airlift C–54 on what was known as the Mary Ann Site. This section of the overhaul was known as Station No.3 and work included engines, instruments, electrics, sheet metal and fuel cells. Engine cowls have been removed for a check on whether a replacement is needed, dependent on the hours run since the last check. (*via Aldon P. Ferguson*)

Right: Looking down the line of maintenance docks during night overhaul operations of the airlift Douglas C–54 Skymaster transports maintenance project at Oberpfaffenhofen air depot near Munich. (*67952 US Air Force*)

Below: Special lights assist mechanics in making accelerated maintenance inspections in order to keep the maximum number of aircraft in the air with food and coal for blockaded Berlin. All crew chiefs and radio operators have been assigned to ground maintenance duties, leaving only the pilot and co-pilot to handle the plane while in the air. (*68357 AC US Air Force*)

Above: The engines – Pratt & Whitney R–1830–92s – on this Douglas C–47 Skytrain are inspected and any minor adjustments made during the unloading of this USAF transport named *The Fabulous Texan* at Tempelhof, Berlin during the blockade. The transport is from the European Air Transport Services (EATS) with serial 43–16143.
(*67611 US Air Force*)

Left: Ground crews worked non-stop night and day to keep the aircraft transports up to their maximum serviceability. Shown here are maintenance crews at the huge Rhein-Main air base near Frankfurt performing a routine check on a USAF Douglas C–47 from the European Air Transport Service (EATS), 43–15346. On the left is M/Sgt Bert F. Grey, with the aircraft's crew chief; T/Sgt William W. Browne is on top of the Twin Wasp engine and M/Sgt Homer D. May is crouched on the engine stand.
(*67991 AC US Air Force*)

Below: Ramp scene at Rhein-Main air base, Frankfurt, with a Douglas C–54 Skymaster parked during engine change. The Pratt & Whitney (P&W) Twin Wasp R–2000 1,450hp 14–cylinder series of air-cooled radial engines were used to power the C–54, ranging through the R–2000–3, –4, –7, –9 and –11 models. As the Skymaster was not in service prior to the airlift in the European theatre, spares including engines had to be airlifted from the USA utilising the new huge C–74 Globemaster I transport. To accommodate 200-hour maintenance and overhaul the USAF depot at Burtonwood in the United Kingdom was enlarged and became part of the operation.
(*Douglas*)

Above: The US forces employed on the airlift utilised military overhaul facilities in Europe and the USA for their aircraft and engines. The RAF employed civil contractors in the United Kingdom, especially for the overhaul and maintenance of the large fleet of Douglas Dakota transports used. Field Aircraft Services based at Croydon Airport, Surrey, had a huge overhaul facility for the Pratt & Whitney R–1830–92 Twin Wasp engines which powered the ubiquitous Dakota. This photo shows part of the Croydon facility with engines in various stages of overhaul. (*AP Photo Library*)

Right: Lost in the shiny reflection on the nose of this airlift Douglas C–54 Skymaster is the rest of the caption: '1,000th AIRCRAFT THROUGH BURTONWOOD', recording the 1,000th transport to be processed for its 200-hour overhaul on 18 June 1949. Burtonwood was re-activated in October 1948 when the 59th Air Depot Wing was moved in to undertake the task.
(*Wayne Jordan via Aldon P. Ferguson*)

Below: Busy hangar scene at Lübeck. Some six hours after landing with a faulty engine this Dakota was fully serviceable, air tested and ready for another flight to Gatow with supplies. The Dakota was powered by two well-proven 1,200hp Pratt & Whitney R–1830–92 fourteen-cylinder Twin Wasp radial engines. As the RAF operated nearly 2,000 Dakotas over the years there was no lack of spare engines. (*R1764 MoD AHB*)

British Civil Airlift

As the daily tonnage requirements for Berlin grew, the RAF soon realised they could not spare sufficient aircraft to provide the necessary airlift capacity, and it was for this reason that British civilian aircraft were chartered to bridge the gap. However, before this stage was reached a need arose for specialised aircraft for the carriage of petrol, and as Flight Refuelling already had Avro Lancastrian tankers in use, three of them were chartered by the Air Ministry. The first flight was made by this company on 27 July 1948 when tanker G–AKDR piloted by Captain D. Hanbury flew a load of petrol direct to Berlin from its home base at Tarrant Rushton in Dorset. Operations continued using Bückeburg on a temporary basis. No-one at the time could have envisaged the magnitude of the task by the end of the year.

During mid-1948 the Foreign Office appointed British European Airways (BEA) under its chief executive, Sir Peter Masefield, as the managing agent for the civil airlift, working under the control of the RAF which exercised full direction of the civil effort through BEA staff. It involved co-ordinating and supervising initially seventeen airlines operating into RAF Gatow with what was termed a motley collection of aircraft including Douglas Dakotas, Handley Page Haltons, Avro Lancastrians, Tudors and Yorks, plus an Avro Lincoln, Bristol 170 Freighter/Wayfarer, Consolidated Liberator, Vickers Viking and three Short Hythe flying boats, all involved in a massive operation which accounted for about a quarter of the total airlift. With the exception of BOAC and BSAA the civil fleet was composed of aircraft belonging to private charter companies based in the United Kingdom.

The charter superintendent of BEA, Colonel G. Wharton, was present at discussions held between the Foreign Office, the Air Ministry and the

Below: Scottish Airlines was one of the first to take part in the civil airlift, contributing two Dakotas G–AGWS and G–AGZF to RAF Fassberg on 4 August 1948, both operating as freighters until 27 August when they were withdrawn. G–AGWS completed fifty-one sorties to Berlin flying over 126 hours and airlifting over 175 tons (178 tonnes) of freight. G–AGZF flew fifty sorties in over 127 hours carrying over 172 tons (175 tonnes) of freight. The company also employed three Consolidated Liberators on the humanitarian operation. (*AP Photo Library*)

Above: A total of nineteen British civil Dakotas were involved in the airlift including G–AKAY *Ecclesia*, contributed by Sivewright Airways, albeit for a very short period. Commencing 19 October 1948 the Dakota flew freight operations from Fuhlsbüttel–Hamburg but was withdrawn on 15 November. It completed thirty-two sorties in eighty-seven flying hours carrying 116 tons (118 tonnes) to Berlin. (*AP Photo Library*)

Ministry of Transport & Civil Aviation. As a result the civil airlift came into being on 4 August 1948 utilising a small fleet of ten Dakotas to be based at Fassberg and three Short Hythe flying boats operating from Finkenwerder on the River Elbe. One Handley Page Halton of Bond Air Services and one Consolidated Liberator from Scottish Airlines were also chartered and based at Wunstorf alongside the Avro Yorks operated by the RAF. The large ventral pannier on the Halton was capable of holding 8,000lb (3,629kg) making this RAF Halifax conversion a useful transport. Overall direction of the civil airlift was assumed by Mr E.P.Whitfield, BEA manager Germany, who had the added task of the day-to-day operation of the scheduled passenger and cargo service BEA operated from Northolt to Berlin via Hamburg. On 1 April 1949 Whitfield was appointed by Peter Masefield as head of BEA Airlift Division. As agent for the Foreign Office BEA had responsibility for the civil airlift until it ended on 16 August 1949. Six airfields were being used to fly supplies into Berlin and two BEA liaison officers were on each base to cover a twenty-four-hour operation, often working under considerable pressure.

The first night sortie was flown by Bond Air Services Halton G–AIOI piloted by Captain Treen, landing at Gatow just after three a.m. During the first twenty-four hours of operations this transport carried out five return flights between Wunstorf and Gatow. Initial problems for the civil aircraft were many. Radio crystals for the frequencies in use in the corridors into Berlin had to be obtained from the RAF. At Fassberg the British Army, which was responsible for the loads for each aircraft, requested that the civil Dakota carry the same standard

payload of 7,480lb (3,393kg) as the RAF Dakota. The civil Dakota carried 6,000lb (2,722kg) and clearance from the Air Registration Board (ARB) was necessary and approved by 16 August.

Early in August Flight Refuelling moved from Bückeburg to Wunstorf to join the solitary Halton, a type which proved satisfactory, and eventually forty-one were involved. The Liberator G–AHDY was withdrawn not having produced a high enough standard of serviceability. On 28 August all the civil Dakotas moved to Lübeck to join the RAF Dakotas. The flying boat operation out of Finkenwerder, a pure daylight operation as no night landing facilities either on the River Elbe or Lake Havel were available, was proceeding smoothly. The three civil Hythes – G–AGER, G–AGIA and G–AHEO – of Aquila Airways were operated by ex-Coastal Command Sunderland personnel who knew many of the RAF crews operating the Sunderland flying boats. Excellent aircrew morale and good serviceability produced three sorties a day and the payloads improved from 9,982lb (4,528kg) at the start to 10,900lb (4,944kg) by the end of August, and 12,400lb (5,625kg) by the end of October.

With the approach of autumn and winter the dwindling stocks of domestic fuel in Berlin were causing anxiety. An adequate tanker force was an urgent necessity. Fortunately the Avro Tudors of BSAA were available but it took time to convert them from passenger airliners to tankers. Five Mk V aircraft were scheduled to commence operation on 1 January 1949 but only three were in use by 7 January, the remaining two not arriving until early February. A number of Haltons were converted as tankers and a fleet of thirty-one had been planned for 1 January 1949, but on that day only eleven, increasing to twenty on 14 January, were available. By the end of the month the tanker force consisted of five Tudors, nine Lancastrians and the aforementioned Haltons. A daily target of 220 metric tons had been set, but because of delays in tanker conversion only 148 tons were achieved. With the increase in the number of tankers operating, the liquid fuel loading arrangements at Wunstorf and Schleswigland became sorely taxed.

Bond Air Services operated twelve Halton tankers, these being a mixture of ex-BOAC and ex-RAF Halifaxes, the latter purchased from the huge RAF maintenance unit located at Hawarden, Cheshire. The cost was £200 per aircraft and some had as little as twelve hours on the airframe since manufacture. Six were bought, all of them the type used by airborne forces as transports. One, G–AIOI, was written off at Tegel on 15 February 1949. The company became closely associated with Freddie Laker's Southend-based Aviation Traders who had purchased the entire fleet of BOAC Haltons, of which a number were converted for use on the airlift and leased to Bond Air Services. Of these Halton G–AHDP was written off at Schleswigland on 9 April 1949. On 14 November 1948 Bond moved tanker operations from Wunstorf to Hamburg, operating until 15 August 1949 when the company was withdrawn from the airlift. It completed 2,577 sorties flying 6,425 hours and airlifted 17,131 tons (17,405 tonnes) of mixed fuel.

Generous terms were offered to civil aircraft operators to induce them to devote as many surplus aircraft as possible to the humanitarian airlift. The terms offered for four-engined aircraft were £70 per hour plus fuel and maintenance – in other words all the operator had to do was to provide the aircraft and crew. The officials of the ever-impecunious British South American Airways under its general manager Air Vice-Marshal D.C.T. Bennett, were tempted by the offer, the only problem being that the company had virtually no surplus aircraft. At this juncture, however, it was learnt there were five Avro Tudor V aircraft – the model with the lengthened fuselage – in an advanced state of completion, and provided they were used exclusively on the Berlin airlift, the Ministry of Supply was prepared to sell them at £30,000 each which was less than half the normal price. BSAA jumped at the opportunity and in the three months between November 1948 and February 1949 it took delivery of G–AKBZ, G–AKCA, G–AKCB, G–AKCC and G–AKCD. At the company's engineering base at Langley near Slough, four were stripped of all furnishings and converted to tankers for the airlift. They were fitted with bomber fuel tanks mounted on edge inside the fuselage and used for the carriage of fuel oil. The company's participation in the airlift lasted until 10 August 1949 when the last of the BSAA Tudors was withdrawn.

Meanwhile the three BSAA Tudor Is G–AGBZ, G–AGRH and G–AGRJ were hurriedly pressed into

Below: British Overseas Airways Corporation (BOAC) provided three of its Dakotas fleet – G–AGIZ, G–AGNG, G–AGNK – to the airlift for a short period. They flew eighty-one sorties into Berlin, involving 224 flying hours, and carried 294 tons (299 tonnes) of freight. The three Dakotas arrived at Fuhlsbüttel–Hamburg on 20 October 1948 and had been withdrawn by late November. Shown is BOAC Dakota IV G–AGNG ex-RAF KK216 c/n 26997 which completed thirty-three sorties in just over eighty-nine flying hours, and carried over 119 tons (121 tonnes) of freight.
(*Aviation Photo News*)

Above: Westminster Airways contributed two Dakotas and four Halton transports to the civil airlift, the Dakotas being G–AJAY and G–AJAZ. On 4 August 1948 G–AJAZ began flying sorties from Fassberg, moving to Lübeck twenty-four days later, this being followed by a move to Fuhlbüttel–Hamburg on 5 October. By the end of the month G–AJAY had joined the operation, both aircraft being withdrawn on 23 November after completing a total of 228 sorties to Berlin with freight. G–AJAY completed forty-four sorties in 127 flying hours carrying nearly 160 tons (163 tonnes), and G–AJAZ flew 184 sorties in 527 flying hours carrying 664 tons (675 tonnes). (*AP Photo Library*)

service in order to train a number of young first officers to be acting captains on the airlift. Two of the three – G–AGRH and G–AGRJ – were used as freighters and completed 231 sorties, while G–AGBZ was converted to a tanker completing 517 sorties and airlifting 4,392 tons (4,462 tonnes) of fuel. By this time Don Bennett had bought two Tudors – a Mk 2 G–AGRY and a Mk V G–AKBY – and formed his own company, Airflight. Tudor 'Baker Yoke' was converted as a tanker with five large fuselage tanks, capable of airlifting nine tons of diesel fuel. Based at Wunstorf, on Sunday, 31 October 1948 Bennett was scheduled to pilot Tudor V G–AKBY with Ken Hagyard as co-pilot and Vic Brennan as radio officer. It was an eight a.m. take-off with a drizzling overcast and Bennett noticed the three elevator locks on the port side had already been removed. It was only when barely airborne that Bennett realised the elevators had jammed – the starboard elevator lock had not been removed, nor had it been correctly applied. The Tudor could neither climb nor descend. Bennett's only hope was to stay within the Wunstorf circuit and attempt to line up on the runway. This he did three times, but always at an oblique angle. At last, with the GCA controller monitoring the fourth and successful attempt, Bennett put the huge Tudor on the runway, black smoke streaming from the tyres, which were flattened to the wheel rims. It had been a human error, the responsibility for which Bennett alone accepted. Both man and machine had stood

the test. Tudor G–AKBY completed a total of 415 sorties flying 1,156 hours and carrying over 3,575 tons (3,632 tonnes) of varied fuels.

With the approach of autumn in 1948, it became obvious that the Russians intended to continue the blockade through the winter months, so plans were made for a considerable expansion of the British civil fleet. The dwindling stocks of liquid fuel in Berlin were still causing anxiety, and clearly the assembling of an adequate tanker force was becoming a matter of urgent necessity. The Handley Page Halton, the civil version of the World War Two Halifax bomber, was now obsolete. Fortunately, the Avro Tudor became available and the first of the type to join the airlift was Mk II G–AGRY, operated by Air Vice-Marshal D.C.T. Bennett and his newly-formed Airflight company, and this arrived at Gatow on 3 September 1948 carrying a load of 20,000lb (9,072kg).

British South American Airways commenced operations from Wunstorf later in the month with two Tudor Mk I freighters G–AGRH and G–AGRJ. During September reinforcements were received at Wunstorf in the shape of two Halton freighters of Skyflight – G–AIWP and G–AKBR – two Wayfarers of Silver City – G–AHJC and G–AHJO – and two Vikings of Transworld Charter – G–AHON and G–AHOT. The Wayfarers were the passenger version of the Bristol 170 Freighter and were introduced as a stop-gap until the latter type could be made available. It was required to transport awkward loads such as vehicles, snowploughs, and rolls of newsprint. Its large loading doors in the nose, and the great cubic capacity, made it suitable for this type of load.

With the approach of the first winter the months of October and November saw an increased influx of both RAF and USAF aircraft, bringing fresh difficulties for the civil airlift. Re-deployment of the civil fleet was necessary once more. On 6 October the civil Dakotas were moved from Lübeck to Fuhlsbüttel, Hamburg, now a 'Plainfare' base but not up to airlift standard. Work was already in progress on the construction of a new 1,950yd (1,783m) concrete runway parallel to the existing 1,600yd (1,463m) PSP strip. This new runway was opened for use on 21 December 1948. In addition a well-illuminated tarmac loading apron was built and a new system of airfield lighting installed. This system was similar to that at Gatow and Wunstorf and was highly effective. The approach path was 3,000ft (914m) long, consisting of white lights every 100ft (30.5m) from the end of the runway intersected every 600ft (183m) by a crossbar of sodiums. The down-wind end of the runway was marked by a green threshold bar and the runway itself was defined by white contact lights along each side. The Fuhlsbüttel installation also had an interesting experiment in the additional refinement of a line of green lights down the centre of the runway, and this was found particularly useful by pilots for checking immediately any incipient swing on night take-offs with a heavily laden aircraft. Although this lighting system was a

useful visual landing aid, in bad visibility it could not be regarded as a substitute for the normal radio or radar blind approach aids. The lack of GCA at Fuhlsbüttel was therefore a serious handicap in bad weather, especially as the alternative BABS – Blind Approach Beacon System – was out of action for long periods due to the beam being affected by construction equipment in use on the airfield.

Civil Dakota operations at Fuhlsbüttel continued to increase in number, with three BOAC Dakotas – G–AGIZ, G–AGNG and G–AGNK – arriving on 20 October. Shortly after Dakota sorties were restricted due to congestion at Gatow, and between 10 and 23 November all the Dakotas were withdrawn. In October the contract for Skyflight's Haltons G–AIWP and G–AKBR was cancelled due to unsatisfactory results by the company. World Air Freight joined the airlift on 6 October with Halton G–AKGZ which unfortunately became the first civilian aircraft casualty when two days later it broke its back following a swing on take-off at Gatow. There were no casualties. Further reinforcements were provided by Bond Air Services who by this time had increased their unit to four Haltons; Eagle Aviation contributed two Halifaxes, Airwork a Bristol Freighter. Three Halton freighters of Lancashire Aircraft Corporation arrived on 16 October, and the first Halton tanker from Lancashire on 30 October. In the meantime, Airflight had received a second Tudor Mk V and both their aircraft G–AGRY and G–AKBY were operating as tankers.

A milestone was reached on 11 November when

Below: The part aircraft from the Lancashire Aircraft Corporation played in the airlift became almost legendary, and by the end of the humanitarian operation the company had undertaken more sorties than any other charter company, with the exception of Flight Refuelling. It was 16 October 1948 when the company positioned three converted Handley Page Halifax tankers, known as the Halton in civil guise, at RAF Wunstorf. Shown is Halton G–AHWN fitted with freight pannier at RAF Celle. It completed seventy-eight sorties to Berlin as a freighter and 230 after it had been converted as a tanker.
(*Doug Pirus*)

Above: On 4 August 1948 a Bond Air Services Handley Page HP 70 Halton I transport commenced flying sorties on the airlift from Wunstorf. The company was closely associated with Freddie Laker's Aviation Traders who had purchased the entire fleet of BOAC Haltons, many being converted for use on the airlift and leased to Bond. The single Halton was soon joined by eleven others which carried essential supplies to Berlin. On 14 November 1948 Bond moved their operations with the Halton freighters from Wunstorf to Hamburg, and sorties continued until 15 August 1949 when the company was withdrawn from the humanitarian operation after flying a total of 2,577 sorties in almost 6,500 flying hours, carrying over 17,131 tons (17,405 tonnes). Shown in BOAC livery is Halton I G–AHDU c/n 1372/Sh18C ex-RAF PP310 which on the airlift completed 363 sorties, flew over 854 hours and carried 2,505 tons (2,545 tonnes). (*Aviation Photo News*)

the civil airlift reached its centenary of operations, and in these first 100 days, 3,944 sorties had been flown and 18,585 short tons lifted.

Initially a dozen civil-registered Douglas Dakota transports were provided to support the airlift by seven British charter companies, comprising Air Contractors – G–AIWC, G–AIWD, G–AIWE; Air Transport Charter (Channel Islands) – G–AJVZ; Ciros Aviation – G–AIJD, G–AKJN; Kearsley Airways Limited – G–AKAR, G–AKDT; Scottish Airlines – G–AGWS, G–AGZF; Trent Valley Aviation – G–AJPF; and Westminster Airways – G–AJAY. Later another seven aircraft were added: British Nederland Air Service – G–AJZX; British Overseas Airways Corporation – G–AGIZ, G–AGNG, G–AGNK; Hornton Airways Limited – G–AKLL; Sivewright Airways Limited – G–AKAY; and Westminster Airways – G–AJAZ.

The second phase of the civil airlift operations from 12 November 1948 to 19 February 1949 began with a further major deployment of the civil fleet. The Haltons were moved out of Wunstorf to make room for three Yorks from Skyways, which joined the operation on 16 November, and the arrival of BSAA's Tudor tankers. Bond Air Services and Eagle Aviation moved their freighters to Fuhlsbüttel, Hamburg, between 14 and 20 November, and Lancashire moved their Haltons to Schleswigland on 24 November. With the withdrawal of the Vikings and Wayfarers during this period, Wunstorf became exclusively an Avro base for Tudors, Lancastrians and Yorks.

Unfortunately, civil operations from Schleswigland were handicapped by three major factors. Firstly, as the base was sited on the Baltic coast it suffered from low stratus and sea mist. Secondly, it was the most distant airlift base from Berlin involving more flying hours, and this reduced the operational utilisation rate. In addition the strict operation height of 6,000ft (1,829m) laid down created serious problems for the Haltons which were not equipped with proper wing de-icing equipment, and allied to this problem was low ground temperatures: as the aircraft were parked out in the open, it could take half an hour to defrost them before start-up, and ice would often form again by the time the aircraft were lined up for take-off. The third main problem at Schleswigland was the desperate shortage of hangar space, having a serious effect on maintenance, especially in the winter months. During December 1948 the civil aircraft fleet as a whole was faced with an even more serious problem. A directive from HQ No.46 Group, dated 17 December, laid down that British aircraft not fitted with Rebecca could only fly VFR conditions. In winter months the chances of finding VFR conditions in the corridors to Berlin were remote, and neither the Haltons nor the Bristol Freighters were equipped with the essential radio aid.

By the middle of November 1948, with the growth of the civil airlift combined with the increase in USAF C–54 Skymasters operating out of Celle and Fassberg, the air bases in Berlin began to reach saturation point, despite the opening of Tegel. Consequently it became more than ever imperative that the allocation of sorties to civil aircraft should be fully utilised day and night. The AOC No.46 Group agreed to the allocation of a separate block of beacon times to the civil aircraft at each base instead of allocating the beacon times to the base en bloc. It was the responsibility of the resident BEA co-ordinator to split the civil allocation between the various companies on the basis of aircraft strength and sortie potential.

The month of December was marred by the first civil casualty. On 8 December Captain Clement Wilbur Utting, the senior pilot of Airflight, was knocked down and killed by a lorry on the tarmac at Gatow in the early hours of the morning as he was walking back to his Tudor aircraft. He was a short distance ahead of his crew when it happened. He died shortly afterwards in the Spandau hospital. It was particularly tragic that this very competent and keen aircraft captain should have met his death in this manner. In spite of strenuous efforts by the police, the culprit was never found.

On 15 December the flying boat base at Finkenwerder was closed and the three Short Hythes withdrawn. The three aircraft – G–AGER *Hadfield*, G–AGIA *Haslemere*, and G–AHEO *Halstead* – had completed 265 sorties and carried

1,400 tons (1,422 tonnes). The risk of ice forming on the Havel Lake was growing daily. Despite doing an excellent job, their speed made it increasingly difficult to fit them into the Gatow traffic pattern. On the following day an Avro York of Skyways made the 5,000th landing by a civil aircraft in Berlin.

By the end of 1948 the fuel stocks in Berlin were practically exhausted, and from the first day of 1949 the beleaguered city became entirely dependent on fuel supplies carried by the British civil aircraft fleet. A daily target of 220 tons (223 tonnes) had been planned but because of delays an average of only 148 tons (150 tonnes) was delivered. A fleet of thirty-one tankers was planned to be on line by 1 January 1949, but only eleven aircraft were available on that date. It increased by twenty by 14 January but was still four aircraft short by the end of the month.

Flight Refuelling had increased its strength to seven tankers. Skyways introduced two Lancastrians, and a new company, British American Air Service, positioned two Halton tankers at Schleswigland. Westminster provided one Halton on 20 January while Lancashire increased its fleet to ten tankers during the month. The twenty-seven-strong fleet was made up of five Tudors, nine Lancastrians and thirteen Haltons. With seventeen

Below: The decision to end the civil airlift was taken in July 1949, and on 15 August the last civil sortie was flown by Eagle Aviation Halton G–AIAR piloted by Captain Villa. It carried 14,400lb (6,532kg) of flour into Tegel, landing at 0145 hrs on 16 August. Eagle operated four Haltons on the airlift and shown here is G–AIAR ex-Halifax HP 70 C VIII PP326 c/n 1388.
(*J.M.G. Gradidge*)

Above: On 4 August 1948 a Bond Air Services Halton G–AIOI started the civil airlift flying a night sortie from Wunstorf to Gatow. The company operated twelve Haltons on the airlift and on 14 November the fleet of freighters was moved to Hamburg. Shown is Halton G–AIOI which was written-off in an accident at Tegel on 15 February 1949 after completing 129 sorties. (*J.M.G. Gradidge*)

freighters in service the civil fleet numbered forty-four. This increase in the number of tankers put pressure on the liquid fuel loading arrangements at Wunstorf and Schleswigland. At Wunstorf the system was operated by British Army personnel from No.1 RASC Unit as a stop-gap until a more permanent underground installation could be built. The bowser system took forty minutes to load 2,100 gallons (9,547 litres) of diesel oil into a Tudor. Between the period 21 January and 21 April there were fifty instances when sorties were lost due to an excess of forty minutes taken to fuel aircraft. During the same period 2,827 tanker sorties were flown from Wunstorf, so the loss represented only 1.8 per cent. Schleswigland had a fixed underground system installed with eighteen refuelling bays, supplied by six pumps fed from ten tanks. Major Craig, commanding the RASC detachment on the base, modified the system so that the fuelling time for a Halton was reduced from twenty to twenty-five to twelve to fourteen minutes, making additional sorties possible.

At Gatow, during the summer of 1948, two gasolene tanks with a capacity of 11,000 gallons (50,006 litres) each were available. As only two tankers at a time could be handled, plans were drawn up for new fuel storage facilities. Work was started by the RAF at the end of September 1948 and completed in March 1949, with five large underground tanks being built and connected to eighteen defuelling points. These were so arranged that fourteen tanker aircraft could be defuelled at the same time, utilising two hoses on each. From the terminal the fuel was pumped to storage tanks erected above ground level holding 108,000 gallons (490,979 litres) in total. Tanker lorries then distributed it, and at a later date fuel was pumped to Havel Lake at the rate of twenty-two tons of petrol or thirty tons of diesel per hour via a pipeline that had been used as part of PLUTO – Pipeline

under the Ocean – for the Normandy beach-head in 1944. At Havel fuel was loaded on to barges, five of which belonged to a shipping company based in Rotterdam. The *Catalonia* was moored permanently at Havel wharf and was utilised as a storage vessel for US forces in Berlin; MVs *Algeria, California* and *Sardinia* were used to transport fuel to depots in Berlin until April 1949, when the *Sardinia* was transferred to ferry fuel arriving at Tegel; and the MV *Polonia* was sent to Charlottenburg in January 1949 to act as a fuel storage vessel for the Berlin power station. A sixth vessel, the Belgian-owned *Grimsel,* was used to ferry fuel from the *Catalonia* to the Wannsee for use by the US occupation forces. The six barges made a total of ninety-one trips, carrying 38,000 tons (38,608 tonnes).

During the whole of the operation, Shell Aviation Service were in charge of the installation at Gatow and handled no fewer than 7,312 tankers with a load of 14,020,090 gallons (63,736,731 litres) discharged. Defuelling operations at Tegel were controlled by the US Standard Oil Company. On the aircraft side, the main difficulty was that individual companies developed their own ideas on tank layout and connections, and expected the ground organisation to cope with each aircraft as a separate problem. This resulted in a multitude of adapters and hoses of different shapes and sizes having to be made available at the defuelling points at Gatow and Tegel. There was a turn in the tide for the civil airlift which included the passing of the liquid fuel target, a daily average of nearly 400 tons (406 tonnes) being achieved during the last week of February 1949.

During the evening of 15 January the civil airlift suffered a second fatal accident on the ground. A German driver was taking six ground engineers of Lancashire Aircraft Corp. to the dispersal area when he carelessly drove his vehicle on to the perimeter track in front of a RAF Hastings at Schleswigland. It was impossible for the pilot to avoid a collision and three engineers and a German were killed by one of the aircraft's propellers. Another engineer was injured.

Lancastrian G–AHJW of Flight Refuelling struck a hill, near Thruxton on 23 November 1948 during a return flight from Germany to its home base at Tarrant Rushton in Dorset for a routine overhaul. As the tanker was also carrying airlift aircrew as passengers who were returning home on leave, the death toll was heavy, eight including three aircraft captains losing their lives.

The first fatal civil aircraft accident on the airlift occurred on 15 March 1949 when Skyways York G–AHFI stalled on final approach to Gatow and spun into the ground. On a return flight from Tegel, Halton G–AJZZ of Lancashire struck some high ground on 21 March 1949 near Schleswigland during a BABS let down. The sole survivor of the crew of four was Radio Officer Hamilton who was thrown forty feet over a hedge; despite being seriously injured he managed to walk nearly two miles back to the airfield to report the position of the crash. After a prolonged stay in hospital, Hamilton returned to flying duties on the airlift.

Halton G–AKAC of World Air Freight crashed nine miles west of Oranienburg in the Soviet Zone on 30 April 1949 during a return flight from Tegel. Captain Lewis and his three crew were killed. On 10 May 1949 Flight Refuelling Lancastrian G–AKDP force-landed at dawn seven miles west of Ludwigslust in the Soviet Zone. Captain Tucker carried out a skilful landing, and although the

aircraft was written off the crew were only slightly injured. After treatment in a Russian hospital they were allowed to return to the British Zone. An RAF salvage party recovered the wreckage.

On 1 June 1949 Halton tanker G–AKBJ of Lancashire was written-off in a landing accident at Tegel. On 10 June Halton freighter G–AITC of World Air Freight was seriously damaged in a landing accident at Fuhlsbüttel, Hamburg. The aircraft was later repaired. Two days later, on 12 June, Halton tanker G–ALBZ of Lancashire was written-off in a landing accident at Tegel, the crew escaping with slight injuries except for the radio officer who spent nearly a month in hospital. Skyways York G–ALBX was written-off following a crash-landing on 19 June in a field shortly after take-off from Wunstorf. Lancashire tanker G–AKFH was written-off on 26 June in a landing at Gatow when the aircraft was completely destroyed by fire, the crew escaping with only superficial burns. Other accidents involved two Haltons, two Lancastrians and a Liberator.

A major concern during May 1949 was the state of the Tegel runway, which had been constructed of brick rubble overlaid with tarmac, and the continuous landings had created undulation in the surface. The uneven surface caused aircraft with conventional type undercarriages to bounce on landing, and in crosswind conditions caused a swing to develop. This problem seemed to affect the Haltons and during eight months of operations into Tegel, no fewer than six Haltons were written off as a result of undercarriage failures, and five more were seriously damaged.

Below: Two huge Avro Tudor I aircraft, operated by British South American Airways (BSAA), G–AGRH and G–AGRJ, converted as freighters, commenced airlift operations during September 1948 from RAF Wunstorf. Averaging a load to Berlin of 20,600lb (9,334kg) the Tudors were carrying more than any other airlift aircraft. A total of 231 sorties were completed before the aircraft were withdrawn from use in August 1949.
(*A.V. Roe via Roy Day*)

Above: General Tunner introduced a policy to the effect that no aircraft crew member could leave the vicinity of his aircraft after arrival at Gatow and Tempelhof. The pilots were briefed for the return flight on the spot by an Operations Officer and a Weather Briefing Officer, and to satisfy the inner man a mobile snack bar liberally stocked with hot coffee, hotdogs and doughnuts appeared on the flight line. The photo shows a typical US mobile snack bar with what appears to be a British civilian aircraft crew waiting to be served.(*AP Photo Library*)

On 12 May 1949 the blockade of Berlin by the Soviets was lifted. At this point the civil contribution to the airlift had amounted to 86,252 tons (87,632 tonnes) in just over ten months, but the civil operation carried on for a further three months. At midday on 22 May the civil tonnage passed the 1,000-ton (1,016 tonnes) daily mark for the first time, 1,010 tons (1,026 tonnes) being airlifted in 133 sorties. A second milestone was reached on 31 May when Lancastrian tanker G–AKDR piloted by Captain D. Hanbury of Flight Refuelling landed at Gatow carrying the 100,000th ton (101,600 tonnes) of cargo flown by the civil fleet to Berlin. To mark the occasion the AOC-in-C, Air Marshal T.M. Williams, flew in the aircraft. It was also a great occasion for both Captain Hanbury and G–AKDR as they had flown the very first civil cargo, consisting of fuel, to the beleaguered city on 27 July 1948.

On 13 July the civil operations at Schleswigland came to an end with cancellation of the contracts for Lancashire, British American, Scottish Airlines and Westminster. Four days later the four Lancastrian tankers of Skyways, operating from Wunstorf, were withdrawn followed by the lone Lincoln tanker G–ALPF of Airflight on 21 July. The liquid fuel requirement had dropped to a daily 140 tons (142 tonnes), and the airlift of fuel ended on 15 August with BSAA carrying 100 tons (102 tonnes) and Flight Refuelling forty tons (41 tonnes) daily, before being withdrawn.

The final decision to end the civil airlift was taken at the end of July 1949, and on 15 August the last civil sortie on Operation 'Plainfare' was flown by Halton G–AIAP Captain Villa of Eagle Aviation. It carried 14,400lb (6,532kg) of flour landing at Tegel at 0145 hrs local time on 16 August. This brought to an end the greatest transport operation in the history of civil aviation. Its success was due to the skill, energy and devotion of the aircrew and ground personnel of no fewer than twenty-three British charter companies plus BOAC and BSAA. A total of 103 aircraft were in use at different periods. Between October 1948 and July 1949, the aircraft engaged at any one time varied between thirty-one and forty-seven. In just over a year, the fleet flew 21,921 sorties to Berlin and carried a load of 146,980 tons (149,332 tonnes).

In his farewell message to the civil airlift, the Air Officer Commanding-in-Chief said: 'We have all learned many lessons from this operation not least of which has been the ability to co-operate, live and work together under all conditions of weather and emergency.' Civil aircraft companies had certainly proved that they could operate effectively in a military operation, in full co-operation with the RAF. If, however, they are required to undertake a similar task at a future date, it is to be hoped that the lessons learned on Operation 'Plainfare' will not be forgotten, so that the civil fleet will develop its full potential much earlier than was possible on this operation.

Above: On 2 January 1949 the first of five Avro Lancastrian II tankers operated by Skyways Limited arrived at RAF Wunstorf to commence airlifting petrol and diesel oil to Berlin. Each aerial tanker was equipped to carry 2,100 gallons (9,547 litres) of diesel or 2,500 gallons (11,365 litres) of petrol. The Lancastrian tankers were withdrawn on 17 July 1949 having amassed a remarkable total of 1,655 sorties during 4,359 flying hours. Shown is Lancastrian tanker G–AKFH *Sky Scout* at RAF Celle. It flew 196 sorties to Berlin. (*Doug Pirus*)

Above: Airflight withdrew two Tudors at the end of May 1949 and replaced them with a single Avro Lincoln G–ALPF on a two-week trial. It arrived at Wunstorf on 24 June 1949 completing one flight as a freighter before conversion to tanker, flying its first flight as such on 30 June carrying 2,500 gallons (11,365 litres). It completed forty-five sorties as a tanker, accumulating over 115 flying hours and carrying a total of over 425 tons (432 tonnes) of badly needed fuel for the power stations in Berlin. (*J.M.G. Gradidge*)

Above: A rare photo showing Flight Refuelling ex-Lancaster Mk III G–AHJW converted as a tanker which completed forty sorties on the airlift flying over 130 hours and carrying 221 tons (225 tonnes) of fuel into Berlin. It was destroyed on 22 November 1948 when it hit high ground near Thruxton while on a return flight to its home base at Tarrant Rushton, Dorset, for routine overhaul. The aircraft was carrying airlift aircrews as passengers, returning to the United Kingdom on leave, the death toll being eight which included three aircraft captains. (*AP Photo Library*)

Right Top: British European Airways based at Northolt maintained a daily scheduled passenger and cargo service from Northolt to Berlin via Hamburg throughout the airlift. Two Vickers Vikings of BEA, including G–AHPP, were used during the airlift, mainly to transport supplies including fuel for BEA vehicles based in Berlin. (*J.M.G. Gradidge*)

Right Bottom: On 10 November 1948 Airwork positioned one of its Bristol 170 Freighter aircraft at Hamburg to commence flying sorties on the airlift. This was G–AHJD, which completed fifty-eight sorties. It was joined briefly by Freighter G–AICS which flew sixteen sorties. Four of the Bristol 170 type were operated by Silver City on the airlift, being useful for carrying abnormal loads. In one day on 9 December 1948 G–AGVB carried a total of 76,400lb (34,655kg) of food, machinery, Red Cross supplies and other goods from RAF Wunstorf and Hamburg to RAF Gatow, Berlin. (*AP Photo Library*)

Below: The British civil contribution to the airlift was greatly enhanced by the introduction of four Avro Tudor V aircraft operated by British South American Airways (BSAA) registered G–AKCA/B/C/D and used as tankers operating out of RAF Wunstorf with effect from January 1949. The highest number of sorties was accomplished by G–AKCA with 529, involving over 1,432 flight hours and carrying a total of over 4,480 tons (4,552 tonnes). The photo shows a BSAA Tudor V tanker parked at RAF Gatow with station HQ in the background. (*AP Photo Library*)

Above: Berlin required thirty-eight tons (39 tonnes) of salt per day. Salt was a difficult commodity to transport in aircraft as it ate through alloys and cables causing severe damage to the control systems. Initially, until Lake Havel froze over, Short Sunderlands of the RAF and later three Short Hythe flying boats from Aquila Airways were used. They were treated to resist the corrosive action of salt water during manufacture. Shown here is Hythe G–AGER of Aquila Airways which only completed six sorties to Berlin carrying a grand total of just over thirty-two tons (32.5 tonnes). (*AP Photo Library*)

Above: Scottish Airlines from Prestwick supplied three ex-RAF Lend-Lease Consolidated Liberators to the airlift, G–AHZP as a freighter and two, G–AHDY and G–AHZR, as tankers. Shown here is G–AHZR which completed 148 sorties, flew over 489 hours and carried over 1,182 tons (1,200 tonnes). The tankers were converted during the winter of 1948 re-commencing on the airlift on 19 February 1949, operating out of Schleswigland. They were withdrawn on 12 July after completing 381 sorties. Liberator G–AHZR is seen parked at RAF Gatow. (*AP Photo Library*)

Below: Avro Lancastrian tankers of Flight Refuelling, which operated a fleet of twelve on the airlift, are seen parked at RAF Wunstorf. On 31 May 1949, after the blockade of Berlin had been officially lifted, Lancastrian tanker G–AKDR piloted by Captain D. Hanbury carried the 100,000th ton (101,600 tonnes) flown to Berlin by the civil aircraft fleet. This aircraft completed 526 sorties, flew 1,472 hours and airlifted 3,070 tons (3,120 tonnes). (*R1828 MoD via Bruce Robertson*)

Above: Two airlift veterans from the RAAF, Air Vice-Marshal David Evans (centre) and Wing Commander C.S. 'Dinny' Ryan (right), seen talking to Group Captain Bobby Robson RAF, the Station Commander at Gatow on 22 June 1980. The occasion was the delivery of a RAAF Dakota, a gift from the Australian government, for the Berlin Airlift Memorial Museum. 'Dinny' Ryan flew the air corridors into Berlin 240 times during the airlift as a signaller on RAF Dakotas. (*Air Marshal David Evans RAAF*)

Commonwealth Aircrew

There were two great advantages in including aircrew from the Commonwealth to assist with the airlift. Firstly, Australia, New Zealand and South Africa still operated the ubiquitous Douglas Dakota in relatively large numbers and had plenty of wartime operationally-trained aircrew. Secondly, at the time the airlife commenced in 1948 there were a number of aircrew from Dominion air forces serving a tour with No.24 (Commonwealth) Squadron based in the United Kingdom. The squadron was equipped with the Douglas Dakota and the Avro York, and it was April 1947 when it adopted 'Commonwealth' in its title and from then on had aircrews from South Africa, New Zealand, Canada and Australia merging with the RAF on its strength. When Operation 'Knicker' came into force there were two RAAF crews captained by F/Lt R. Carlin and J. Cornish already serving on the exchange with the VIP squadron.

The RAF Dakota squadrons were the first to be involved in 'Knicker', later Operation 'Plainfare', and by 29 June 1948 the entire sixty-four Dakotas in RAF Transport Command were concentrated at Wunstorf. Two days later they were joined by the first of fifty-six of the heavier four-engined York transports. From Wunstorf the Australians from No.24 Squadron flew either as complete RAAF crews or as composite crews with other squadrons. Flight Lieutenant Cornish's crew in particular had some unusual experiences. During the night of 21 September 1948, a York MW288 preparing to take off in front of them at Wunstorf crashed after suffering an engine failure. Due to the intensity of airlift traffic at that time, the shocked Australians took off in turn as if nothing had happened, while the crashed York and its five-man crew burned nearby.

On 19 July 1948 the distinction of flying the 3,000th sortie into Berlin, an event of major political and moral significance due to the international media attention it received, also fell to Flight Lieutenant Cornish and his RAAF crew. One of the Australian York co-pilots, Flight Lieutenant Mal Quinn, eventually became a captain and transferred to Lübeck where he flew Dakotas with an RAF crew. Unfortunately, he and his crew were killed in Dakota KJ970 during the night of 22 March 1949 while attempting to land at Lübeck in bad weather. The Dakota crashed in communist territory, but with surprising humanity, which invariably marked their actions in similar incidents,

the Soviets recovered the bodies and handed them over for burial. F/Lt Quinn, the only RAAF fatality on the airlift, was buried with joint RAF and RAAF honours in the British war cemetery at Hamburg.

As the airlift became more organised, No.24 Squadron, with its small complement of Australians, returned to the United Kingdom and resumed normal VIP duties. Against this background, 29 August 1948 saw ten RAAF Dakota transport crews, five each from Nos. 36 and 38 Squadrons – forty-one airmen in all – arrive in the United Kingdom for attachment to the RAF. Under the command of Wing Commander C.A. Greenwood, the Australians were initially based at RAF Bassingbourne, Cambridgeshire, where for a week they were re-checked on their instrument flying and issued with 'green cards'. This training was not free of incident as navigator Flt Lt Ken Staib recalled: 'On 7 September 1948 F/Lt Berriman and I were in the crew of Dakota C IV KN520 with an RAF captain undergoing let-down training at Bassingbourne when the aircraft made a single-engined wheels-up landing. It was a good landing and we and the aircraft escaped serious injury.'

On 10 September the RAAF crews were flown to Lübeck to join not only RAF aircrews but also aircrew from South Africa and New Zealand. Airlift flying commenced on 15 September when the Australians, as an un-numbered squadron of the RAAF, flew their first cargoes to Berlin. These initial sorties were uneventful and the Australians fitted well into the RAF flying routine. Originally it had been intended that the Australians would take their own Dakotas to the United Kingdom, but the RAF stock in storage was sufficient. The RAAF crews were told they would be away from home for about six weeks, but it was fourteen months. The Dakotas normally flew from Lübeck to Gatow in blocks of eight aircraft. Freight loads were generally either sixty-seven bags of coal or large rolls of newsprint totalling 6,710lb (3,044kg). Fresh and dehydrated vegetables were also carried regularly. These were unloaded by German labour in fewer than three minutes, but it naturally took much longer to unload the bigger aircraft. During November and December 1948 Lübeck Dakotas were directed into Tegel despite its being only partially completed. Where possible, on the return journey the aircraft carried export goods or passengers out of Berlin.

Above: Dakota aircrew from the South African Air Force joined the Commonwealth contingent to assist in the Berlin airlift. Shown with a RAF Dakota are Major Blaauw in the doorway with Flying Officer Jenkins RAF, Lt Joubert on the steps, and Lt Ralston, Lt Delport, Lt Pretorious and Captain Barlow at ground level.
(*Major Dave Becker, SAAF Museum*)

In November 1948 conditions were often impossible for flying and many sorties were cancelled due to the presence of thick fog. Consequently the monthly tonnage of supplies delivered dropped to a disappointing 3,800 tons (3,861 tonnes). By December this had increased to 4,500 tons (4,572 tonnes), while in the first two months of 1949 the figure increased to 5,500 tons (5,588 tonnes). In March the figure was 6,300 tons (6,400 tonnes) and in April 8,000 tons (8,128 tonnes). With these large tonnages being despatched from West German airfields as quickly as aircraft could be turned round, it was essential that cargoes were loaded into the aircraft intended. Occasionally loads were inadvertently loaded into the wrong type of aircraft, but this was usually detected on the ground. On one occasion, a RAF Dakota was loaded with a cargo intended for a York weighing some 11,500lb (5,216kg) instead of 5,500lb (2,495kg). Before the error had been detected the Dakota was on its take-off run, staggering into the air with its Pratt & Whitney Wasp engines on emergency boost. It did just clear the airfield's perimeter fence before joining the circuit to make a safe landing. Disaster, in this case, was only averted by a miracle and the crew's skill.

A problem which could have had more serious consequences related to landings at Lübeck in marginal weather conditions using the BABS – Blind Approach Beam System. Crews regularly entered East German airspace as an approach of two or three miles was necessary and the runway was only 1,500 yards (1,372m) from the Russian border. The Soviets appeared to take no action against these incursions, of which they must have been aware.

It is significant to note that along with the South African and New Zealand crews, the Australians were the only aircrew to be permanently employed on the airlift. The RAF crews were seconded for periods of a month or so before returning to normal RAF Transport Command duties; the American crews were also relieved on a regular basis. By the conclusion of the RAAF's participation in the airlift each of the Australians had on average completed between 220 and 240 sorties to and from Berlin. At a farewell function in the Officers' Mess at Lübeck the RAAF were presented with two wooden carved kangaroos. In one, a slide from the pouch listed the number of sorties flown and the total weight of cargo lifted by the Australians; in the other pouch the following was recorded: 'Plus 50,000 beers and benedictines'.

The RAAF made their last flight on 19 September after which the crews returned to the United Kingdom where they were accommodated at RAF Manston, Kent, until departing for home in a RAF York on 20 October 1949. The RAAF's contribution during the airlift was significant. Apart from their presence demonstrating Commonwealth solidarity, the crews of the un-numbered Dakota squadron flew 2,062 sorties, carrying 15,623,364lb (7,086,711kg) of freight and 6,964 passengers involving a flight time of 6,041.5 hours. To this impressive total must be added the contributions of the RAAF-crewed Yorks whose payload capacity was twice that of the Dakota. On arrival at Darwin each of the RAAF airlift veterans was handed a copy of the Air Force HQ signal A763 after it had been read to them by the Air Officer Commanding North Western Area. It stated: 'I wish to express my congratulations and my appreciation to the very fine performances by all members of the 86 Wing Berlin Airlift Detachment in Europe. Your hard work, efficiency and devotion to your duty have set a fine example to the Royal Australian Air Force and have contributed greatly to the prestige of your Service and your country.' This signal came from Air Marshal Sir George Jones, the Chief of the Air Staff.

As with the RAAF, aircrew from the RNZAF were also serving on the exchange with No.24 'Commonwealth' Squadron when the airlift commenced, and flew both York and Dakota aircraft to Berlin. Group Captain R.J. Cohen RNZAF was Senior Air Staff Officer (SASO) at HQ No.46 Group RAF Transport Command on a two-year exchange duty from New Zealand. For 'Nugget' Cohen the historic airlift was his most challenging assignment. The responsibility he carried as SASO was considerable. His RNZAF career had in fact been centred around aircraft operations; it was a field in which he excelled and the airlift benefited from his talents.

Initially, three RNZAF crews commanded by Flight Lieutenant C.J. Fraser flying Dakotas from Lübeck agreed the airlift involved the most difficult flying they had ever undertaken. During an average twelve-hour working day they would accomplish three flights to Berlin. The aircraft carried mainly coal, but in addition loads included newsprint, cigarettes and a host of miscellaneous goods. On the return flight they often carried children suffering from malnutrition. Flying conditions in the corridors were frequently very unpleasant and during the long winter months icing was a real problem. There was no room for error as there were always aircraft ahead and astern, above and below, too many, too close for anything but meticulous accurate flying. Attached to the RAF

Below: On 10 July 1948 VIP York MW100 from No.24 Commonwealth Squadron based at Bassingbourne in Cambridgeshire flew the Prime Minister of Australia, Mr Chifley, from the UK to Gatow. It was a mixed crew, seen in this photo: the pilot, Sq/Ldr A.R. Middleton, and the flight engineer were RAF; co-pilot and navigator RAAF; wireless operator SAAF; and a second navigator was from the RNZAF. A similar York flew the British Foreign Minister, Ernest Bevin, to Germany on a tour of airlift bases in 1949. (*Sq/Ldr A.R. Middleton RAF*)

during the airlift, the New Zealanders, who were drawn from No.41 Transport Squadron based with Dakotas at Whenuapai, flew over 1,500 tons (1,524 tonnes) of coal into Berlin between October 1948 and July 1949. They departed from New Zealand in September 1948.

On 30 April 1949, the New Zealand Minister of Defence, Mr F. Jones, announced that replacement crews had been selected and would sail from Wellington for Europe in the *Mataroo* on 14 May. After completing some six months on the airlift two of the three relief crews would be based in the United Kingdom for a two-year exchange tour with No.24 'Commonwealth' Squadron.

The RNZAF flew their last sortie to Berlin on 11 August 1949. On its completion the Commanding Officer at Lübeck presented F/Lt C.L. Siegert with a handsome plaque to commemorate the event. The plaque records that the RNZAF carried 1,577 tons (1,602 tonnes) of coal into Berlin on 473 flights.

Prior to 18 September 1948 the airlift for most in South Africa had been but another move in the Cold War between East and West in Europe, and all in the South African Air Force were amazed at the way the RAF and the USAF had commenced flying supplies into Berlin when all other methods of entry had been sealed off by the Russians. It appeared to be a very large undertaking well accomplished, and SAAF personnel read about the airlift with the interest one accords a major event taking place 6,000 miles (9,656km) away. However, on 18 September the airlift suddenly became a very personal matter for thirty-one

members of the SAAF as they were informed that the time had come for Dakota crews to add a contribution to it. These crews had been on stand-by for nearly a month, as the lifting of the blockade had appeared imminent until negotiations between the military governors in Berlin finally broke down.

The SAAF contingent of ten crews comprising twenty-one officers and ten NCOs under the command of Major D.M. van der Kaay assembled in Pretoria from air bases all over South Africa. The pilots had been selected for their wide range of Dakota experience and all had completed green ticket courses, which authorised flying in adverse weather conditions, such as would certainly be encountered during winter in Europe. They departed South Africa in two batches by air on 22/23 September 1948 and were informed that relief crews would be available in four to six months' time.

On 26 September the SAAF aircrew arrived at Oakington, Cambridgeshire, then transferring to Bassingbourne for training which commenced two days later. Instruction was given on the Gee system of grid navigation, Rebecca-Eureka homing, and the BABS let-down procedure. A great deal of single-engine flying and bad weather circuits at 300ft (91m) took place by day and night. On occasion the instructor would cut an engine shortly after take-off, ask for a bad weather circuit with visibility of 1,000 yards (914m) and then remark as the aircraft was being landed, 'You have no landing lights, no flaps and your port tyre has burst,' just to make things a bit more complicated. But it all helped to build up a pilot's confidence in his ability

Below: Daily scene at Tegel airfield located in the French sector of Berlin showing RAF Dakotas being unloaded after arrival from Lübeck. All the RAF Transport Command Dakotas on the airlift were pooled, although crews were naturally keen to retain their squadron identity. Fortunately the Dakota was available in large numbers, so it was not necessary for the Commonwealth elements to supply any aircraft, just Dakota crews. (*Major Dave Becker, SAAF Museum*)

to handle the Dakota under the most treacherous conditions. All this training was handled by instructors from No.24 'Commonwealth' Squadron.

It was 18 October when the SAAF aircrew left Bassingbourne to fly to Lübeck to operate on the airlift. The northern corridor was used by the Dakotas operating from Lübeck, Yorks from Wunstorf, Skymasters from Celle and Fassberg, and Hastings from Schleswigland. These aircraft either landed at Gatow in the British sector or at Tegel in the French sector. In addition Sunderlands operated for a while from the River Elbe near Hamburg to Havel Lake near Gatow. The southern corridor was used by USAF and US Navy Skymasters, the main load-carrying aircraft on the airlift with their ten-ton cargoes, based at Rhein-

Main and Wiesbaden near Frankfurt and operating to Tempelhof in the American sector. The central corridor was used by aircraft leaving Berlin, this ensuring a constant circular stream of traffic entering and leaving the city throughout the twenty-four hours of the day, except when the weather was very bad and flying temporarily ceased.

Different types of aircraft were briefed to fly at different altitudes, which ensured that aircraft with the same cruising speed would fly at the same height. These altitudes changed according to weather conditions and the general overall plan. Dakotas commenced flying at 4,500ft (1,372m), then when Tegel was used it became 1,000ft (305m), and when Dakotas reverted back to Gatow 5,500ft (1,676m) was allocated. The airlift provided a vast exercise in the techniques of using transport aircraft to their maximum capacity on a precision operation. Timing was all-important. The block system of operating aircraft from the airlift bases was used, whereby, in the case of aircraft destined for Gatow, each base was given a block time for its aircraft to be over the Fronhau beacon, the focal point of entry to Berlin along the northern corridor and sited twelve miles north of Gatow. Aircraft normally took off at three-minute intervals in good weather or five-minute when GCA was being used for landing at Gatow. A deadline was set for the last aircraft in the block to be airborne. If for any reason an aircraft was unable to get off on time, its flight was cancelled for that particular detail.

First trip to Gatow for the SAAF aircrews was in mid-October with an experienced RAF crew in order to become familiar with the procedures and the route. An operations hangar had been earmarked at Lübeck for use by aircrews and ground crews and it contained steel lockers for the storage of flying clothing and parachutes. A long desk displayed all the flight information and here the RAF Form F.700 was ready for signature. A dining room provided meals day and night. On a large blackboard behind the operations desk were listed the respective crews with aircraft number, times to take off and set course, height to fly and, most important of all, the time to be over the Fronhau beacon. For each block, normally comprising five or six Dakotas, a standard flight plan was worked out by the navigators of the first aircraft using either the latest meteorological wind velocity forecast, or a wind velocity recorded by an aircraft on a previous block flight. Speeds used were 110 knots (201kph) and a rate of climb of 500ft (152m) per min, and 125 knots (229kph) for straight and level flight. There was no need for special briefings before flights as all the necessary information was contained in a special briefing sheet issued to each crew.

Below: The first contingent from the South African Air Force consisted of ten Dakota crews comprising twenty-one officers and ten NCOs under the command of Major D.M. van der Kaay. The picture shows Lt Jack Hosking, radio operator, in the door, Lt Peter Norman-Smith, pilot, and Lt Attie Bosch, navigator. Between them they completed 140 sorties out of Lübeck flying supplies to Gatow. The '83' on the tail of the Dakota is the aircraft identification number for loading purposes. (*R1767 MoD AHB*)

Above: Scene at Gatow on 19 July 1948 – an all-Australian York crew known as the 'Kangaroos' with No.24 Squadron from Wunstorf. Their flight, in an aircraft loaded with 1,600lb (726kg) of flour, was the 3,000th sortie by the RAF. The photo shows John Cornish, the RAAF pilot, being greeted with roses and a talisman by Fraulein Gretel Schoenrock from the economics division at Wilmersdorf City Hall. The talisman was a tiny winged wooden horse. (*Sq/Ldr E.G. Ferguson RAAF*).

At first everything appeared somewhat complicated for the SAAF crews. From the pilot's point of view it was a matter of trying to pick out the main landmarks and to get to know the R/T procedure. For the navigator it was a case of keeping a constant check, either visually or with the aid of Gee, of the track being made good, to ensure the aircraft did not stray out of the corridor and that it arrived over the Fronhau beacon on time, where the maximum latitude allowed was only thirty seconds either way. The Eureka beacon at Fronhau was normally picked up a good way out on the Rebecca set, and at the twenty-mile checkpoint Gatow was called up and instructions were given as to what height the aircraft had to arrive over the beacon. On arrival over Fronhau Gatow was called again and then landing instructions were passed by the airfield controller. After landing, hardly had the aircraft stopped before a lorry drew up to the door and the aircraft was being unloaded by half a dozen German labourers. Usually there were ten other aircraft being unloaded and no time was wasted, the crew having only fifteen minutes to spare for refreshments before it was time to taxi out. It was an amazing sight at Gatow to see the regularity with which aircraft landed and took off with clockwork precision. The variety of types would include Dakotas, Yorks and Tudors. Return to Lübeck was along the central corridor.

On 31 March 1949 the opening of the CPS–5 radar control unit at Tempelhof greatly improved aircraft safety in the approaches and within the control area of Berlin. When GCA conditions were in force at Gatow, aircraft were given instructions all the way from Fronhau on courses to steer, rate of descent and distance from touchdown, and it was very reassuring when pilots broke cloud at 300ft (91m) or less to find the runway straight ahead. In the event of a missed approach, however, aircraft had to return to base as there was no time to bring them into the circuit a second time. There was no GCA at Lübeck so BABS was used when the cloud base was low. This generally necessitated aircraft orbiting the Bargetheide beacon at 500ft (152m) intervals while the airfield controller allowed one aircraft in at a time.

During the afternoon of 5 April 1949 the initial batch of SAAF aircrew completed their last sortie. During the time the contingent had been at Lübeck they had completed 1,240 sorties and carried 4,133 tons (4,199 tonnes) of supplies into Berlin. The second contingent of thirty aircrew under Major J.P.D. Blaauw brought the totals up to 2,500 sorties flown and some 8,333 tons (8,466 tonnes) of goods, mainly coal, carried. The final SAAF crew flew their last sortie to Berlin on 24

August 1949. Six SAAF personnel flew as members of General E. Poole's crew (Poole was the South African military representative in Berlin). As a mark of appreciation for the work the SAAF aircrew had achieved they received two messages of thanks before they departed for home. A message from the Air Officer Commanding No.46 Group read: 'We in 46 Group will miss you. You have fulfilled your task with high skill and invincible determination, which is the   hallmark of the veteran squadrons of the airlift. But what has impressed us most has been your cheerful enthusiasm and your readiness to volunteer for additional missions on your rest days.' A personal message of thanks from the Air Officer Commanding the Berlin airlift read: 'We have all been tremendously impressed by the South African Squadron. Not only have they taken their full share in the task of supplying Berlin, but the selfless devotion of all ranks has been an inspiring example.' It had been a great experience and the SAAF aircrew had made many friends.

Left: The South African Air Force contributed sixty-one aircrew personnel who flew on the airlift with No.46 Group RAF. They accomplished 2,500 sorties to Berlin and carried 8,333 tons (8,466 tonnes) of supplies, mainly coal from Lübeck. The photo shows SAAF pilot Lt Peter Norman-Smith from No.240 Operational Conversion Unit in the doorway of Dakota 'NU–P for Peter'.(*R1768 MoD AHB*)

Below: The South African Air Force Dakota crew who flew the cargo of coal from Lübeck to Gatow on 22 April 1949 which completed the 50,000th short ton from the base. The final sack of coal to complete the load is being handled by a RAF Wing Commander and a supply officer from the Royal Army Service Corps. (*A0363/7 AP Photo Library*)

Right: With No.24 being known as the 'Commonwealth' Squadron, it had a constant exchange of aircrew from Australia, Canada and New Zealand, a number of whom were on the unit when the airlift commenced. The squadron operated VIP Yorks and Dakotas. Seen at Gatow during the airlift are two aircrew from the RAAF. On the left is Flying Officer M. Singleton, flight engineer, with F/Lt J. Cornish, a pilot.
(*Sq/Ldr E.G. Ferguson RAAF*)

Below: Personnel from the RAAF squadron employed on the Berlin airlift from 14 September 1948 to 24 August 1949, seen posed in front of a RAF Dakota. The squadron completed 2,062 sorties airlifting 15,623,364lb of miscellaneous freight, carried 6,964 passengers and flew a total of just over 6,041 hours. This was accomplished with no accidents or incidents.
Back row l to r: F/Lt D.V. Hahn, WO K.F. Barnett, WO R.G. Williams, WO Paddy Grant, WO Bob Bray, WO H.R.D. Johnston, WO D.S. Benson-Inglis, WO Ron Ewin, Flying Officer David Evans, WO V.A. Smith, WO C.S. Ryan, WO 'Blue' Paine, WO Lance Clements, WO D.M. Clark.
Front row l to r: F/Lt D.I. Kuschert, F/Lt T.S. Fairburn, F/Lt Ron Mitchell, F/Lt E.G. Gentle, F/Lt G. Page, Sq/Ldr C.A. Greenwood (Commanding Officer), F/Lt R.S. Murdoch, F/Lt V.B. Cannon, F/Lt T.L. Bourke, F/Lt F.K. Carrick, F/Lt W.R. Berriman. (*R.G. Williams*)

Casualties

Friday, 13 August 1948 is a date many who served on the airlift will remember. It was a day of black scudding low clouds and driving rain. The weather at Wiesbaden was better. Some twenty C–54 Skymasters were airborne heading for Tempelhof, each with three minutes separation, flying at 180 mph. When crossing the Fulda Range station the pilot transmitted his radio call-sign, his time was estimated to the next checkpoint, his altitude and in-flight conditions noted, then forty minutes later he called Tempelhof airways giving a position report and obtaining further information. It was at this point the radar was able to pick up the incoming transports after an identification turn.

The airlift was seven weeks old, but all was not well over Berlin. The cloud base had dropped to the tops of the high apartment buildings surrounding Tempelhof, and a cloudburst obscured the runway from the control tower. The radar could not penetrate the sheets of rain, and both GCA and tower operators had no alternative but to stack the incoming Skymasters, and this was soon extending vertically from 3,000 to 12,000ft. One C–54 had overshot the runway, crashing into a ditch at the end of the field, and caught fire – the crew got out alive. Another C–54, loaded to maximum with coal, landed too far down the runway. To avoid piling into the transport on fire ahead, the pilot braked heavily, blowing both mainwheel tyres. A third pilot coming in low over the housetops saw what he thought was a runway and descended. Too late he discovered he had chosen an auxiliary runway still under construction, and the C–54 slipped in the rubble base for several precarious moments, then ground-looped.

It was chaos all round. On the ground a traffic jam built up as transports came off the unloading line to take off and climb out on the homeward bound three-minute conveyor belt, but were refused permission to take off for fear of collision with the aircraft stacked overhead. Airborne at the time was General William Tunner in his personal C–54 45–549, destination Tempelhof for a presentation ceremony. Later Bill Tunner revealed that the real success of the airlift stemmed from that Friday the thirteenth. The General and his team of experts introduced one standard and constant set of flight rules to govern all aircraft at all times in all weather conditions.

Earlier, in July 1948, six USAF C–47 Skytrains and two C–54 Skymasters had been involved in major accidents, two of which occurred in flight, three on final approach to land, and three on the ground. One of the C–47s hit a block of flats while on the approach to Tempelhof on 25 July, this being reported in the *Berlin Observer*: 'the third accident and the second fatal crash of the 7,231 flights logged in "Operation Vittles" occurred early Sunday morning when a C–47 piloted by Lt Charles H. King of Britton, South Dakota, and Lt

Below: On 2 May 1949 another newly developed US transport aircraft joined the airlift operating out of Rhein-Main. This was the third Boeing YC–97A Stratofreighter 45–59595 flown by Strategic Air Command crews. It airlifted more than one million pounds, some hundred and fifty thousand kilograms, of freight in twenty-seven flights into Berlin. Despite being experimental it proved the aircraft's design by carrying bulk coal, loaded by a conveyor belt. Unfortunately it had to be withdrawn in May 1949 after its undercarriage was damaged during a very heavy landing, bursting the tyres. (*MAP*)

Above: Casualties to both military and civil aircraft involved in Operation 'Plainfare' were inevitable, most RAF transport aircraft being salvaged under various categories. This RAF Dakota KN424 was just one. It joined the airlift in 1948 and on 20 October while taxying out for take-off from Lübeck loaded with three tons of coal for Berlin, the RNZAF pilot braked heavily and KN424 tipped up on its nose. On 9 November after recovery it was declared Cat E and reduced to spares. (*via Dennis Usher*)

Robert W. Stuber of Arlinton, California, crashed into the street in front of an apartment building in the Berlin-Friendenau district. Both the pilot and co-pilot were killed instantly.' Another C–47 crashed in a field on the approach to Wiesbaden, while one C–47 and two C–54s were involved in minor accidents.

The month of August claimed major accidents to three C–47s and two C–54s with one of the C–47s catching fire in mid-air, while two C–54s were wrecked in landing accidents. In September the figures were five C–47s and a single C–54 involved in serious accidents, with three of each type suffering minor accidents. By the end of 1948 USAF transport aircraft had been involved in thirty-eight major and twenty-one minor accidents, the latter including one of the five Fairchild C–82A Packets which had a tyre rupture on landing in December. On 6 December a C–54 laden with coal for Berlin crashed three kilometres from its base at Fassberg killing three members of the crew.

Fortunately not all crashes were fatal. On 14 September 1948 Captain Kenneth W. Slaker of Lincoln, Nebraska, and Lt Clarence Steber of Mobile, Alabama, were en route from Wiesbaden to Berlin in a C–47. Just after entering Soviet airspace both engines quit and the two pilots baled out. Steber was picked up by the Soviet military and returned to US authorities in Berlin a day later. Slaker, with the aid of friendly East German civilians, simply walked back through the Iron Curtain to West Germany.

By November 1948 two squadrons – VR–6 and VR–8 equipped with R5D– Skymasters had joined the airlift arriving at Rhein-Main on 10 November, and VR–6 flew its first flight to Berlin two days later. On 15 November R5D– BuNo.56545 piloted by Lt-Cdr Stephen Lukacik overran the runway at Tempelhof and was burnt. The squadron lost its second R5D– BuNo.56502 on 11 December 1948 when on return from Berlin to Rhein-Main it flew into high ground approximately fifteen miles from base. The pilots, Lt Joseph L. Norris and Ensign George H. Blackwood, were seriously injured while the skipper, Harry R. Crites, was killed. The transport was making an instrument approach when it struck high terrain near Königstein just after midnight.

There were many incidents both on the ground and in the air involving RAF and British civilian aircraft. Many aircraft parked on an airfield with two or three times as many ground vehicles of all shapes and sizes naturally do not mix very well unless strict procedures are adhered to. During the first full month of the airlift in 1948 there were twenty-seven assorted incidents involving RAF Transport Command aircraft. At Wunstorf a German driver of a RAF vehicle hit a Dakota and damaged the pitot head. An Army driver backing up to a Dakota misjudged the distance and hit the fuselage. At Fassberg a Dakota being parked after unloading was found to have a damaged aileron. An unauthorised airman driving a petrol bowser hit a parked Dakota and damaged the leading edge of the starboard wing. An airlift Dakota landing at Bückeburg swung off the runway and was damaged. F/Lt H.C.M. Holmes was flying a Dakota from Wunstorf to Gatow when a piston in the port engine failed. He jettisoned half his load and managed to return to Wunstorf on one engine. Another aircraft, also bound for Gatow, had a fuel leak and returned safely on one engine. Carburettor trouble caused a Dakota to return to Wunstorf shortly after take-off. En route to the United Kingdom Dakota KN641 had to make a forced landing at Schiphol, Amsterdam, on 21 July 1948,

and KN252 crashed on 24 July after a fire in the air near Fassberg.

The RAF evacuated more than 10,000 children, elderly Germans and displaced persons selected by the Berlin City Health Department in passenger-carrying airlift aircraft, mainly Dakotas. On 7 April 1949 Flying Officer David Evans of the RAAF was captain of a Dakota carrying twenty-two passengers out of Gatow. Immediately after take-off at 200ft the port engine lost power; at 400ft the engine failed completely. The pilot feathered the propellers on the dead Twin Wasp engine, carried out a circuit, and accomplished an excellent single-engine landing in spite of a strong wind, taxying the Dakota clear of the runway. F/O Evans received a green endorsement from Group Captain A.J. Biggar, station commander at Gatow. David Evans retired as Air Marshal from the RAAF having flown 231 sorties for a total of 744 hours – 442 by day and 322 at night.

There were casualties among airlift personnel too. On 19 September 1948 Avro York MW288 crashed at Wunstorf after engine failure following a night take-off, the crew of five was killed. Dakota KP233 crashed on 17 November 1948 at night inside the Russian Zone near Lübeck when making an approach to land in bad weather. Three of the crew were killed immediately and F/Lt J.G. Wilkins, the navigator, died of his injuries later. A similar accident involved Dakota KN491 on 24

Below: Douglas C–54 45–514 of the US Air Force which almost skidded into the street beyond Tempelhof's runway on 'Black Friday', 13 August 1948. It overshot the runway, crashed into a ditch and caught fire. The crew were saved. A second C–54 loaded to maximum with coal touched down too far down the runway. To avoid piling into the C–54 on fire ahead the pilot braked heavily and blew two tyres. A third aircraft mistook the auxiliary runway still under construction for the duty runway, and ended up in a ground-loop. It was a bad weather day with cloud base on the top of the apartment buildings on the approach, while a sudden cloudburst obscured the runway from the tower.
(*Landesbildstelle-Berlin*)

Above: There was always danger in the air with so many flights in and out of Berlin. The sheer number of flights in often fatigued aircraft plus overworked aircrews was bound to result in some casualties. On 30 July 1948 the *Berlin Observer* reported: 'The third accident and the second fatal crash of the 7,231 flights logged in "Operation Vittles" occurred early Sunday morning when a Douglas C–47 Skytrain 43–49534 piloted by Lt Charles H. King and Lt Robert W. Stuber crashed in the Berlin-Friedenau district. Both the pilot and co-pilot were killed instantly.'
(*Landesbildstelle-Berlin*)

January 1949 when approaching to land at RAF Lübeck in bad weather; the signaller, Sgt L.E. Grout, and seven passengers were killed, and two crew members and a number of others injured. A third Dakota, KJ970, crashed at night in the Russian Zone on finals to Lübeck in bad weather; the pilot, F/Lt M.J. Quinn RAAF, and navigator, F/O K.A. Reeves, were killed immediately while the signaller, Sgt. A. Penny, died of injuries later.

On 16 July 1949 Hastings TG611 crashed on take-off from Tegel during the early morning; the crew of five was killed including Sgt. J. Toad from the Glider Pilot Regiment, who was the co-pilot. Earlier, on 5 April 1949, Hastings TG534 caught fire on start-up and broke in half on the hardstanding dispersal at Schleswigland. Included in the official listing of RAF aircraft involved in accidents and requiring salvage by either No.1 or No.2 Mobile Repair & Salvage Unit (MRSU) during 1949 were the following Hastings: TG525 at Tegel on 6 February; TG522 also at Tegel on 4 April; TG510 at Schleswigland on 19 May; and TG573 also at this base on 18 July. The list includes one RAF Sunderland flying boat, SZ582, on 9 October 1948 at Finkenwerder on the River Elbe, and one Lancaster PA380 on 10 March 1949 at Schleswigland.

Two versions of the Avro York were operated by RAF Transport Command on the airlift, one the passenger/freighter-carrying 15,000lb (6,804kg) and the other the freighter-carrying 16,500lb (7,484kg); usage was approximately two to one in favour of the freighter. At one time the York was carrying sixty-one per cent of the RAF contribution and made only forty-two per cent of the movements. They were ideal transports for the cargoes destined for Berlin, and on several occasions proved to be the only suitable aircraft for airlifting awkward return loads out of Gatow. This workhorse suffered its fair share of accidents as follows: MW315, 28 July 1948, Gatow; MW199, 3 August, Wunstorf; MW245, 25 September, Wunstorf; MW305, 10 October, Gatow; MW270, 11 November, Wunstorf; MW234, 22 November, Wunstorf; MW246, 3 December, Gatow; MW300, 14 December, and MW238, 15 December, at Gatow; MW232, 15 January 1949, Gatow; MW299, 25 January, Gatow; MW297, 19 March, Wunstorf; MW308, 29 March, Wunstorf; MW271, 7 April, Wunstorf; MW188, 21 April, Gütersloh; MW264, 4 June, Wunstorf; MW145, 30 July, Wunstorf; and MW195, 15 August, Wunstorf. Most were repaired and continued to operate on the airlift.

The ubiquitous Douglas C–47 Dakota had been supplied to the RAF in large numbers during World War Two under the huge Lend-Lease programme, so it was still available in large numbers at the commencement of the airlift. Nine squadrons and the Dakota Operational Conversion Unit (OCU) contributed aircraft which operated in a pool. Naturally there were a number of accidents, as follows: KN213, 22 July 1948, Gatow (survived); KN252, 26 July, crashed Fassberg and written-off; KN507, 3 August, Bückeburg, and struck off charge; KN238, 3 August, crashed Gatow and written-off; KN631, 17 September, Lübeck (survived); KN355, 20 September, Lübeck, and struck off charge; KN523, 12 October, Bückeburg, and struck off charge; KN424, 1 November, Lübeck, and struck off charge; KN521, 6 November, Gatow (survived); KN567; 4 January 1949, Bückeburg, and struck off charge; and KN590, 8 May, Gatow (survived).

On 5 April 1949 Hastings C1 from No.297 Squadron caught fire during start-up at its airlift base at Schleswigland and was destroyed, as these photos show. Initially the Hastings airlifted cargo into Gatow, changing later to Tegel. Being the fastest transport on the airlift it was able to make up time at the Berlin beacons if delayed for some reason. The tolerance from the allocated time was two minutes.
(*Peter Leeds & Geoff Boston*)

Statistics

The Combined Air Lift Task Force (CALTF) was a truly combined force: in addition to the RAF, there were personnel from the Royal Australian Air Force, the Royal New Zealand Air Force, and the South African Air Force, plus a smattering from the Royal Canadian Air Force who had been assigned for duty with No.24 'Commonwealth' Squadron RAF whose aircraft were involved on the airlift. The US Air Force was supported by the two US Navy squadrons who flew the Douglas R5D–, this being the US Navy designation for the Skymaster. On the airlift rivalry was fierce, but it existed between individual squadrons or units rather than between services. When Commander James O. Vosseller's VR–8 Squadron exceeded its quota by over 3,000 tons (3,048 tonnes) in one month with his twelve R5D–s, accolades came from far and wide.

Despite the round-the-clock operation and the adverse weather conditions that persisted during the winter of 1948/49, the airlift accident rate was less than the overall average for the US Air Force. Of the total number of lives lost on the airlift – seventy-nine in all, of whom thirty-one were American – the majority resulted from non-flying accidents. In the huge Operations Room at CALTF HQ, no fewer than fifty analytical charts were kept up to date around the clock providing at a glance at any hour of the day or night a clear overall picture of the entire airlift operation.

By spring 1949, with the daily tonnage still on the increase, the USAF appeared to have the transports needed to maintain the airlift. There were over 150 assorted British aircraft, RAF and civil, some 225 C–54s with an extra seventy-five in the maintenance pipeline and at Great Falls, Montana, with 200 of the 225 in daily service backwards and forwards to Berlin via the corridors. Today, nearly fifty years after the event, the statistics are still only approximate, especially when relating to the number of personnel involved. One source in the USA quoted 45,000 German cargo loaders and airfield workers, 12,000 USAF and 800 US Navy personnel, 8,000 RAF and British Army which included the Commonwealth personnel, 3,000 Baltic state displaced persons, 2,000 US Army Airfield Support Command personnel, and several hundred US, UK and French civilians.

There was always the question of how much longer the humanitarian operation was going to last. The brief use of the large single Douglas C–74 Globemaster on the airlift proved without doubt that the future of air transport lay with large aircraft. The C–74 gave proof of its capability on 18 September 1948 when it was airborne for twenty hours out of the twenty-four, and carried 150 tons (152 tonnes) of supplies into Berlin. Six round-trip flights were made, two more than the usual 'four-block-a-day' schedule operated by the C–54s and C–47s. General Bill Tunner had become an expert on air cargo logistics and modern transport aircraft. Many lessons were learnt from the airlift and Tunner had done his homework and produced a chart which he kept in his office at Wiesbaden. The figures showed that a task force made up of sixty-eight C–74 Globemasters could haul the 5,400 tons (5,486 tonnes) needed in Berlin each day. It took 178 C–54 Skymasters to do the same job, or 899 C–47 Skytrains. With C–74s it would be necessary to make only 5,400 trips a month to maintain the tonnage average, whereas the C–54s would need to fly 13,800 trips, or 39,706 with the C–47. The economics showed that with the C–74 only 16,200 flight hours a month were needed, compared to 42,888 in the C–54 or 158,824 in the C–47. With the aircrew only 180 C–74 crews were needed to do the job, whereas 465 were required for the C–54 and 1,765 for the C–47. There was a similar ratio with maintenance: some 2,700 C–74 maintenance personnel could accomplish the task that would require 4,674 on the C–54s and 10,588 on the C–47s. Finally, you could fly the C–74s on 6,804,000 gallons (30,931,664 litres) of fuel, compared to 8,577,600 gallons (38,994,627 litres) needed by the C–54s, or the 14,294,000 gallons (64,981,953 litres) the C–47s would need.

The paperwork required to support the humanitarian operation was tremendous, involving not only the normal documents to keep aircraft flying, but load sheets and receipts for everything hauled in and out of Berlin, including passengers. At HQ CALTF US civilians were employed to collate all the data, while the Pentagon had teams

Opposite: Berliners of all ages watch from the rubble of their city as yet another Douglas C–54 Skymaster transport lands at Tempelhof during Operation 'Vittles'. By 20 July 1948 the airlift aircraft strength was fifty-four C–54 Skymasters, 105 C–47 Skytrains, forty Avro Yorks, fifty Douglas Dakotas and ten Short Sunderland flying boats. Maximum daily tonnage as of that date was 1,500 tons (1,524 tonnes) (US) and 750 tons (762 tonnes) (RAF). (*Landesbildstelle–Berlin*)

Above: Excellent view of the huge double-cargo-doors fitted to the four-engined Douglas C–54 Skymaster transport which proved to be the workhorse for the USAF during Operation 'Vittles'. Seen on the apron at Tempelhof is a C–54 of the 20th Troop Carrier Squadron which was serving in Panama until ordered to Germany to assist in the Berlin airlift. (*USAF*)

of statisticians monitoring the daily records, and even sent teams to Germany. With the USAF all flight details were completed by the crew chief on Air Force Form 1 which after the flight was processed by Base Operations with hours flown sent to the engineering office and crew flight times to the Air Force Form 5 section, this being a personal record of individual pilots and aircrew divided into day, night, instrument flying etc. The time logged on the AF Form 1 was 'chock to chock', so included taxi time. Different procedures were used by the RAF, dominated by RAF Form 700 which the pilot had to check and sign prior to taking the aircraft over. It had been completed by a senior technician or NCO i/c of the unit. Each member of the aircraft's crew had a personal flying logbook – RAF Form 414 – in which were recorded details of each flight. At the end of each month logbooks were handed in to the unit or squadron HQ for counter-signature by the Commanding Officer or his deputy, usually Wing Commander Flying. Flight times logged were from take-off to landing.

After coal, food was next on the tonnage list, with flour the largest single commodity for foodstuffs. Daily requirement was 646 tons (656 tonnes) plus three tons of yeast. Dehydrated foods soon became more and more important as they came on the market. Dried milk, both whole and skimmed, amounted to over forty tons (forty and a half tonnes) a day, and quantities of fresh milk, eggs, vegetables and meat were airlifted all the time.

It is not generally known that some of the heaviest loads were airlifted out of Berlin. Despite the blockade Berlin's industry, which prior to World War Two had dominated many export fields, managed to recover. Several small factories were active producing cameras, loudspeakers and a very heavy item – electric engines used to haul cars in the coal mines. More as a sign of pride and determination than of economic viability the items were professionally stencilled 'Made in blockaded Berlin'. General Tunner himself revealed that one of the clumsiest items to airlift out of the city proved to be grand pianos, these being the personal property of people moving out of the city. On 11 May 1949 RAF Hastings TG516 flew out a Steinway baby grand from Gatow to Schleswigland. In all some 83,045 tons (84,374 tonnes) of cargo was flown out of Berlin.

US civilian airliners were no strangers to the Berlin airspace. Based at Tempelhof were Douglas DC-3s of American Overseas Airlines (AOA) which operated on feeder routes within Europe. To help Berlin's needy, US citizens sent thousands of CARE (Co-operative for American Remittances to Europe Inc.) packages by civilian air freight. Seaboard and Western Airlines flew Douglas DC–4 Skymasters and carried some of the 20,000 food parcels that reached the city each month. A standard CARE package provided 42,649 calories.

The constant need for spare parts and spare Pratt & Whitney R–2000 engines for the C–54s was critical. When the airlift first started R–2000 engines were shipped to Westover, Maryland, and then airlifted by Slick Airways, a private commercial contract airline, to Rhein-Main two at a time. The engines were packed in heavy metal cans. In a secret report, it was proposed that two C–74 Globemasters from the 521st Air Transport Group, modified to the 165,000lb (74,844kg) gross weight limit, be used on a once weekly flight to Rhein-Main carrying much-needed R–2000 engines. Use of the Globemasters was calculated to save the US government $130,000 over the cost of a contract carrier. The task was assigned to the 6th Air Transport Squadron based at Brookley AFB, Alabama, which flew fourteen R–2000 engines, minus cans, per trip from Kelly AFB, Texas, to Rhein-Main.

Aviation fuel had to be kept flowing to the CALTF air bases. Prior to the airlift the average monthly consumption of aviation fuel in USAF (Europe) was 30,000 barrels (4,770,000 litres). In July 1948, the first full month of the airlift, consumption rose to 82,500 barrels (13,117,500 litres). By January 1949 it was 191,000 barrels (30,369,000 litres), and demand peaked in July 1949 at 291,000 barrels (46,269,000 litres). During the airlift it is estimated that more than 100,000,000 gallons (454,610,000 litres) of aviation fuel (AVGAS) were consumed. The fuel was brought over from the USA in US Navy tankers; the US Naval Transportation Service alone delivered 2,750,000 barrels (437,250,000 litres) or twenty ship loads for use on the airlift. It came into the port at Bremerhaven and then by pipeline or by rail to the airfields. The planning and execution of such a logistical operation was just another example of the type of problem that had to be met and overcome daily. Some of the ex-Luftwaffe bases utilised by the RAF and the USAF had a railhead capacity and bulk fuel installation.

Records were broken daily as tonnage increased. The first big day was US Air Force Day on 18 September 1948 when the US Air Force airlifted 5,582 tons (5,671 tonnes) into Berlin in a twenty-four-hour period. The British added 1,400 tons (1,422 tonnes) making a total of 7,000 (7,112 tonnes). It was an all-out enthusiastic effort that permeated the entire CALTF command. The daily tonnage stayed high through October into November until the weather closed in. The daily minimum supply required and considered necessary for Berlin was revised on 20 October from a total of 4,500 (4,572 tonnes) to 5,620 tons (5,700 tonnes). The items required ranged from baby food to bulldozers. Coal headed the list with a requirement for 3,084 tons (3,133 tonnes).

Towards the end of the airlift in May 1949 there was a requirement to fly in the parts needed for a new power plant being constructed in the British sector of Berlin. Some of the single pieces weighed as much as 32,000lb (14,515kg); one steel shaft alone weighed 28,000lb (12,700kg). By utilising the large C–74 Globemaster and a Boeing C–97 Stratofreighter, plus one of the five C–82 Packets, the parts were flown successfully into the city. Mention must be made of the single YC–97A 45–59595 Stratofreighter which was flown by Strategic Air Command (SAC) crews and which carried more than one million pounds (453,597kg) of freight into Berlin in twenty-seven flights during

Above: Typical flight line scene at Schleswigland, Germany, as Handley Page Hastings transports are loaded with industrial coal destined for delivery to Berlin. The aircraft are TG610, TG551 and TG571. Originally two squadrons of Hastings took part in the airlift commencing November 1948 with No.47 Squadron. A third squadron, No.53, did not re-equip with the type until August 1949 so its time involved on the airlift was limited. (*AP Photo Library*)

Above: Day and night, around the clock, York transports kept up the flow of supplies into Berlin. This photo gives a good impression of the night atmosphere with five Yorks being unloaded. The York contributed no fewer than 233,145 tons (236,875 tonnes) of supplies in 29,000 flights to the humanitarian operation. The payload was increased from seven and a half to nine tons. The last York sortie on the airlift was piloted by F/Lt L.A. Miller of No.511 Squadron, who had as his co-pilot Air Marshal T.M. Williams, AOC–in–C BAFO. Date was 26 August 1949.
(R1821 MoD AHB)

May 1949. However, this unique transport had to be withdrawn after being damaged in an accident while landing at Gatow when all the tyres burst due to the heavy load, the wheel hubs being ground down to the axles.

The estimated miles flown during the airlift were 124,420,813 (200,220,415km) to and from Berlin, involving a total of 277,804 sorties – 89,963 by the US and 87,841 by the British. The operation did not cease on 12 May 1949 when the Soviets lifted the blockade, but went on through to October when the last RAF flight was flown from Schleswigland to Gatow on the 6th by F/Lt D. Harper in a 38 Group Hastings loaded with coal. Of the 394,509 short tons (400,821 tonnes) of foodstuffs, coal and supplies, the Hastings aircraft had airlifted 55,095 tons (55,977 tonnes).

Continuous talks with the Russians on the Berlin issue were getting nowhere, and there were signs that the military strength in the Russian Eastern Zone was being built up. Early in 1949, a directive was issued by HQ BAFO that Operation 'Plainfare' was now regarded as a long-term commitment, and that future planning would be undertaken on the assumption that the airlift was likely to continue for at least another two or three years.

Harassment from the Soviets in the corridors was on the increase during the early weeks of 1949, and earlier on 1 October 1948 US pilots had reported Russian fighter aircraft engaged in firing practice. On that same day the British authorities lodged a strong protest when two Yak fighters buzzed a Bristol Wayfarer of Silver City Airways piloted by Captain Michael Davidson. A US report was compiled giving instances of harassment by various means gathered between August 1948 and

August 1949, revealing the following: searchlights – 103; close flying – 96; radio interference – 82; buzzing – 77; flares – 59; ground fire – 55; flak and chemical laying – 54 each; air-to-ground firing – 42; ground explosions – 39; bombing – 36; air-to-air firing – 14; balloons – 11; UFOs – 7; and rockets – 4. Since the Allies had legal access to Berlin via the three corridors, the Russians could do nothing short of shooting down Allied aircraft, which would constitute an act of war.

The involvement of the British civil aircraft fleet of contractors in the airlift has been well recorded, but it is not generally known that as from 26 July 1948, American Overseas Airlines (AOA) flew 2,366 round trips between Frankfurt and Berlin, carrying 17,242 passengers and 11,356 tons (11,538 tonnes) of cargo and mail. After May 1949, when the airlift was reduced, AOA flew a passenger and freight service to Berlin twice daily. Aircraft used were Douglas DC–3s and DC–4s.

As the spring of 1949 approached it was quite evident from the steadily mounting tonnage in February and March that most problems had been solved, and General Tunner even had all the US transports he needed. But that was no reason for aircrews to rest on their laurels. On 12 March it was recorded that a new weekly tonnage record of 45,644 tons (46,374 tonnes) had been reached. The US Air Force (Europe) revealed that from 1 July 1948 to 1 March 1949 US transports had accomplished 36,797 GCA landings. On the last day of March a new monthly record was set, totals reaching 196,160.7 tons (199,299.3 tonnes). The 61st Maintenance Squadron at Rhein-Main claimed a new USAF record for 154 R–2000 Skymaster engines rebuilt during March. The US Navy squadron VR–8 set an all-time record of 155 per cent efficiency, with an hourly utilisation of 12.2 hrs per aircraft. The GCA crew at Tempelhof handled a transport aircraft every four minutes over a period of six and a half hours on 7 April, setting a new record in sustained operation involving 102 aircraft. The 10,000th GCA landing was achieved at Gatow on 18 June when an Avro Tudor of BSAA was landed by No.5 GCA unit which was commanded by Sq/Ldr S. Halloway. A Skymaster from Fassberg completed an entire round trip to Berlin in one hour and fifty-seven minutes; the turn-around time was fifteen and a half minutes. On 11 April new tonnage figures of 8,246.1 tons were released involving 922 flights for the twenty-four-hour period.

Meanwhile, behind the scenes General Bill Tunner was busy making plans for an even larger operation as a present for the people of Berlin. On Easter Sunday, 16 April, there was to be an Easter parade of aircraft which flew 12,941 tons (13,148 tonnes) of coal, food and other supplies in 1,398 flights to raise the twenty-four-hour operation record to a new high. Airlift aircraft flew 78,954,500 miles and made 3,946 landings and take-offs, and 39,640 radio contacts, making one movement every four seconds during the period. The British contributed 2,086 short tons (2,120 tonnes). Aircraft serviceability remained at 80 per cent, many units claiming 100 per cent utilisation during most of the period.

At CALTF HQ this was a chance for the USAF 'desk jockeys' to join in the operation. General Tunner himself flew to Tempelhof to watch the activities. The Yankee pilots were full of airlift fever.

Douglas C–54 45–555, known as 'Cheerful Earful' because of the variety of ways in which its pilot liked to identify himself, was in rare form. Sometimes '5555' was 'Four Nickels', sometimes 'Four Fivers'. During the Easter parade the pilot broadcast loud and clear: 'Here comes Small Change on the range.' The pilot of 45-477, another C–54 frequently referred to himself as a bundle from heaven, but gave it full treatment on Easter Sunday: 'Here comes 77, a bundle from heaven, with a cargo of coal for the daily goal.' The friendly feud between the C–54s at Fassberg and Celle continued, but with greater determination. When Bill Tunner arrived at Fassberg the actress Constance Bennett was busy down on the flight line with other wives serving coffee and doughnuts. Husband Jack Coulter was watching the station statistics and was proud to announce a ten per cent lead.

Throughout the entire daily operation there was not a single accident or injury. Flight safety had remained paramount. Just under 13,000 tons (13,208 tonnes) of coal had been airlifted and CALTF had come close to averaging one round trip for every one of the 1,440 minutes that make up a day. From Easter Sunday on, the daily haul never fell below 9,000 tons (9,144 tonnes), and it was the view of many that Easter Sunday broke the back of the Berlin blockade. A month later, on 21 May 1949, the Soviets grudgingly reached the conclusion that the land blockade was pointless and surface traffic began to move once more. However, the airlift continued more or less at full capacity for three more months, so building up a stockpile of reserves in the city, just in case. By 1

Below: Aviation fuel of the 100-octane grade, known as AVGAS, was used on the RAF airlift fleet including the Dakotas in the photo. Prior to the airlift the USAF (Europe) average monthly consumption of aviation fuel was 30,000 barrels (4,770,000 litres). It reached a peak during the airlift in July 1949 at 291,000 barrels (46,269,000 litres). More than 100,000,000 gallons (454,610,000 litres) were consumed during the airlift. The US fuel was shipped over on US Navy tankers to the port of Bremerhaven operated by the US Army, and then piped or shipped to the USAF bases.
(*R1773 MoD AHB*)

September it was all over. In a total of 276,926 flights, the Allies had hauled 2,323,067 tons (2,360,236 tonnes) into Berlin. West Berlin was free and the world had been shown what the free nations could do.

The following facts and figures were taken from an official summary prepared by HQ United States Air Forces in Europe (USAFE) published in late 1949, and entitled 'Berlin Airlift – a USAFE summary 26 June 1948–30 September 1949', extent 189 pages. It was originally covered by a Restricted classification, later Unclassified.

Total USAF tons flown into Berlin from 26 June 1948 to 30 September 1949.

Tonnage quoted in short tons =	2,000lb per short ton.
Inbound Total USAF tons hauled =	1,783,572.7
Total RAF tons hauled =	541,936.9
Combined inbound total	2,325,509.6

These are official USAFE figures. However, in 1956 the British Air Ministry reported 695 tons less.

Breakdown of tonnage inbound

	Food	Coal	Others	Total
USAF	296,319.3	1,421,118.0	66,134.6	1,783,571.9
RAF	240,386.0	164,910.5	136,640.4	541,936.9
Total	536,705.3	1,586,028.5	202,775.0	2,325,508.8

Others included weight of passengers and baggage.

Total outbound tonnage from Berlin to British and US Zones.

USAF	45,887.7	
RAF	33,843.1	Total 79,730.8 short tons.

Total passengers airlifted.	Inbound	Outbound	Total
USAF	25,263	37,486	62,749
RAF	34,815	130,091	164,906
Total	60,078	167,577	227,655

Total flights or sorties		Total hours flown	
USAF	189,963	USAF	586,827
RAF	87,606	RAF	Not known
Total	277,569		

Total aircraft miles flown by the USAF, 26 June 1948 to 30 September 1949.

Douglas C–47 Skytrain aircraft miles	7,584,008
Douglas C–54 Skymaster aircraft miles	84,477,853
Total	**92,061,861**

The miles flown by the five Fairchild C–82 Packets, the one Boeing C–97A Stratofreighter, and one Douglas C–74 Globemaster I are unavailable.

There were thirty-one US nationals killed in twelve fatal accidents – eleven in the air and one on the ground.

USAF Officers	22	RAF	18	Germans	7
USAF airmen	6	UK civilians	10		
US Navy Petty Officer	1				
US Army	1				
US Army private	1				
Total	**31**	**Total**	**28**	**Total**	**7**

These figures unfortunately disagree with the number of British casualties appearing on the Airlift Memorial. There were seventy major and fifty-six minor USAF aircraft accidents during the entire airlift period.

Page 189 of the Berlin Airlift chronology dated 18 February 1949 states: '1,000,000th ton is landed in Berlin by a British York aircraft loaded with potatoes.' Concerning the number of USAF aircraft used in the airlift, the cited source states:

After the fleet had been built up to 225 aircraft, the available aircraft engaged in the mission varied between 209 and 228 until final phase-out. When the phase-out began on 1 August 1949, 204 C–54s of the USAF and 21 US Navy R5D– [C–54 type aircraft] were on hand. At the beginning of the airlift, 26 June 1948, there were 102 C–47 aircraft available with a 2½-ton (2.54 tonne) capacity. The C–54s had a ten-ton (10.16 tonne) capacity. From September 1948 to July 1949, five Fairchild C–82 aircraft 'Flying Boxcars' with a 5-ton (5.1 tonne) capacity were used to airlift heavy equipment into Berlin and automobiles out of Berlin. One Boeing C–97A Stratofreighter was used experimentally during May–July 1949. Also one Douglas C–74 Globemaster aircraft with a capacity of 19 tons (19.3 tonnes) was tested. Both the C–97A and C–74 flew approximately eighty-one flights or sorties from Rhein-Main air base to Berlin until returned to the United States. With the arrival of sufficient C–54 aircraft the C–47 aircraft were discontinued in October 1948.

Although the Berlin airlift was officially inaugurated on 26 June 1948, supplies had been flown to Berlin the previous week. Fresh milk was flown to Berlin on 19 and 20 June, 5.88 short tons (5.97 tonnes) of supplies on 21 June; 156.42 tons (158.9 tonnes) on 22 June, and between 23 and 27 June the daily airlift totals averaged about eighty tons (eighty-one tonnes). The biggest tonnage day was on 16 April 1949, the Easter parade, when a total of 12,941 tons (13,148 tonnes) was flown to Berlin in 2,764 flights in a twenty-four-hour period. Of the total, the USAF flew 10,905 tons (11,079 tonnes) and the RAF 2,036 tons (2,069 tonnes). Cargo equalled 600 carloads of railroad transportation, consisting of 2,091 tons (2,124 tonnes) of food, 9,886 tons (10,044 tonnes) of coal, and 964 tons (979 tonnes) of other supplies.

Page 32 from the USAFE history for October 1949 states that the last USAF 'Vittles' flight was on 30 September 1949, when a C–54 aircraft flew to Berlin from Rhein-Main air base with two and a half tons of coal. This aircraft had the following legend painted on its side: 'Last VITTLES flight, 1,783,572.7 tons (1,812,110 tonnes) to Berlin'. The history also states: 'During October, fourteen flights were made to Berlin with cargoes of technical and or special supplies consigned to the airlift. The 60th Troop Carrier Group (Heavy), Rhein-Main air base, was charged with the responsibility of transporting this cargo. On 17 October the last 'Vittles' cargo was transported to Berlin'.

A chronology of the airlift published in the USA commences as follows: 'April 1, 1948: Soviets state that permits will be required for Allied troop movements through the Russian zone. Stockpiling of supplies for occupation forces in Berlin started: "Operation Counterpunch" for the US; "Operation Knicker" for the United Kingdom.'

Below: It is not generally known that the Douglas Aircraft Company converted thirty-eight C–54E–DO Skymasters, stripped of all interior fuselage fittings, in order to carry coal during the Berlin airlift. They were re-designated C–54M–DO. Payload was increased by 2,500lb (1,134kg) to 35,000lb (15,876kg). The photo shows a typical daily scene in Berlin as a C–54 Skymaster makes its approach to land at Tempelhof with some children observing from a building damaged by the ravages of World War Two. (*AP Photo Library*)

Above: On 5 July 1948 the RAF airlift fleet was augmented by the addition of ten Short Sunderland flying boats from Nos.201 and 230 Squadrons from RAF Calshot. The photo shows a Sunderland Mk V VB889 NS–D for Dog from No.201 Squadron unloading foodstuff into barges on Havel Lake, Berlin. Over 1,000 sorties were accomplished, carrying 4,500 tons (4,572 tonnes) of freight including salt and airlifting 1,113 starving children out of Berlin. Winter and the threat of ice brought these operations to a halt on 15 December. (*R1831 MoD AHB*)

Right: Vital coal being unloaded by German labour from a USAF C–54 Skymaster at Tempelhof, Berlin. Much of the coal flown into RAF Gatow was unloaded into barges on the River Havel. When filled the barges, carrying an average of 500 to 700 tons (508 to 711 tonnes) daily, took the coal to Kladow or Westhafen for distribution to industries and homes in the blockaded city. (*Landesbildstelle–Berlin*)

Below: On 14 August 1948 a Douglas C–74 Globemaster I arrived at Rhein-Main, Germany, from the US carrying R–2000 engines required for C–54 Skymasters engaged on the airlift. On 17 August the Globemaster 42–65414 flew into RAF Gatow carrying twenty tons (20.5 tonnes) of flour from Rhein-Main. It was a useful transport but very restricted due to weight on the runways and taxiways. It is shown on arrival at Gatow in the British Zone of Berlin. (*RAF Gatow*)

Above: As each day passed the airlift records were broken giving the official statisticians a heyday. At RAF Gatow RAF aircrew and USAF personnel discuss the latest figures over a cup of tea. At the end of August 1948 the grand total was recorded as 18,048 flights involving a total tonnage of 118,634 (120,532 tonnes). Any quotations on the cost of the humanitarian operation must be treated with caution. The US contribution figure is quoted as being between $200,000,000 and $300,000,000 at a daily figure of $500,000.
(*R1852 MoD AHB*)

Right: The Fairchild C–82 Packet, seen here discharging cargo at Tempelhof during the airlift, was designed around the new concept of a large uninterrupted cargo hold, with direct access for loading at near ground level. To achieve the latter, a twin boom layout was adopted, with the wing mounted high on the deep fuselage, which ended in clam-shell doors at the rear providing for straight-in loading of vehicles up ramps, or of freight from trucks at the same height as the fuselage floor. Gross weight is listed as 54,000lb (24,490 kg) and 32,500lb (14,741kg) empty. (*USAF 68366 AC Douglas*)

Below: Loading sacks of coal into a Handley Page Hastings in preparation for yet another flight to Berlin. It was the first day of November 1948 when the first squadron of Hastings arrived at Schleswigland to join the airlift force, and the first Hastings sortie was completed on 11 November. Many flights with coal were made into Tegel in the French part of the city, as well as Gatow. The return load comprised empty coal sacks.
(*R2045 MoD AHB via Bruce Robertson*)

Top: Eventually, as the airlift became professionally organised, a stockpile of supplies was built up. This is a typical scene in a disused hangar with British Army personnel, assisted by German and foreign labour unloading trucks. In July 1948 69,000 tons (70,104 tonnes) were delivered to Berlin; in August 119,002 (120,906 tonnes); in September 139,623 (141,857 tonnes); and in October 147,581 (149,942 tonnes). In November it declined to 115,588 tons (115,405 tonnes) with the approach of the bad weather period.
(*R1795 MoD AHB*)

Right: Daily scene at Tempelhof, Berlin, during the early days of Operation 'Vittles' with a line of USAF Douglas C–47 Skytrain transports being unloaded. These ubiquitous aircraft carried a wide variety of cargo ranging from engine crates to milk bottles. Nonetheless the unloading crews had to be prepared to handle the unexpected with the same rapidity with which they unloaded the standard loads of sacks of coal and flour. On 30 September 1948 the C–47 was withdrawn from the airlift in favour of the larger Douglas C–54 Skymaster.
(*67950 AC USAF*)

Below: On 30 September 1948 all USAF C–47 Skytrain transports were withdrawn from the airlift and replaced by the larger C–54 Skymaster. The photo shows a typical scene at Tempelhof with a dozen or more Skymasters parked on the large apron. Many USAF squadron aircraft were impressed into service on the airlift and examples in the photo are from the 19th and 20th Troop Carrier Squadrons.
(*USAF via AP Photo Library*)

Victory

On 4 May 1949, after discussions with the United Nations, the four powers at last reached an agreement. All restrictions imposed on traffic to and from Berlin by all parties were to be removed on 12 May, and subsequently the following message was released for broadcast:

> Agreement has now been reached between the three Western Powers and the Soviets regarding raising the Berlin Blockade and the holding of a meeting of the Council of Foreign Ministers. All communications, transportation and trade restrictions imposed by both sides . . . and between Berlin and the Eastern Zones will be removed on May 12 . . .

Promptly at one minute past midnight on 12 May 1949, in the harsh white glare of floodlights, the Russian barriers went up on the *autobahn* at Helmstedt, and the first convoy of British trucks, speeding supplies to the city, poured through.

Though many aircraft and crews were leaving, the airlift was by no means over. Despite the lifting of the blockade, the Allies were determined to ensure a stockpile was maintained so the airlift continued to operate at a reduced rate until 1 August 1949, when it was decided that a gradual rundown should begin, culminating in the withdrawal of all aircraft by the first day of October.

On the first day of August the C–54s from the 317th Troop Carrier Wing ceased operating from Celle. The contracts for the British civilian fleet expired on 10 and 15 August and were not renewed. On 15 August the RAF Dakota strength at Lübeck was reduced to thirty-two, while the twelve Yorks from No.206 Squadron and nine Hastings from No.47 Squadron returned to their UK bases. On 22 August ten Yorks from No.59 Squadron, followed on the 29th by ten Dakotas from No.18 Squadron, also returned to the UK. Seven days later ten Yorks from No.511 Squadron returned home. By 1 September all aircrew from the Commonwealth air forces engaged on the airlift were returned to the UK before taking their long flight home. Also on this day the Combined Airlift Task Force (CALTF) was disbanded and the C–54s from the 60th Troop Carrier Wing ceased operations from Fassberg. Two more RAF Dakota squadrons – Nos.30 and 10, each with ten transports – flew back to bases in the UK on 12 and 26 September respectively. At Schleswigland the Hastings strength had been reduced to sixteen aircraft by 10 October. Five days later HQ No.46 Group was closed down at Lüneburg and personnel returned home. It was the intention to retain two squadrons of Hastings at Fassberg, remaining there as a nucleus just in case the airlift was resuscitated later. However, the aircraft were diverted and based at Wunstorf.

It was 30 September when USAF Captain Perry Immel flew the 276,926th flight in the last airlift C–54 loaded with coal. The sheer statistics and logistics of the operation defied the imagination. A total of 689 aircraft – 441 US, 147 RAF and 101 British civil – were estimated to have flown more than 124 million miles (almost 200 million kilometres) airlifting over 300,000 tons (304,800 tonnes) of supplies at a reputed cost of some $350,000,000 and sixty-five lives. Just a week earlier, on 23 September, RAF Dakota KN652 left Lübeck for Gatow at 1830 hrs. The transport bore the inscription:

Positively the last load from Lübeck – 73,705 tons. Psalm 21, Verse 11. 'For they intended evil against thee: they imagined a mischievous device which they are not able to perform.'

Above: On 28 February 1978 this Handley Page Hastings TG503 transport was placed on permanent display at RAF Gatow, Berlin, as a tribute to the aircraft and personnel who took part in the airlift. Nearly thirty of the type were used to fly supplies including coal into both Gatow and Tegel. A number of sorties were lost due to the crosswind restriction of twenty knots, the type being fitted with a convential tail-wheel undercarriage. On 10 October 1949 the Hastings force at Schleswigland was reduced to sixteen transports. (*RAF Gatow*)

VETERAN DER BERLINER LUFTBRUECKE

DIESE SKYMASTER WAR EINE DER 205 AMERIKANISCHEN C-54 MASCHINEN DIE DIE HAUPTLAST DES AMERIKANISCHEN BEITRAGS ZU DER BRITISCHEN, AMERIKANISCHEN UND FRANZOESISCHEN LUFTBRUECKE NACH DEN FLUGPLAETZEN GATOW, TEMPELHOF UND TEGEL WAEHREND DER BLOCKADE UEBER BERLIN VOM JUNI 1948 BIS MAI 1949 TRUGEN. DIE REKORDTAGESLEISTUNG WURDE AM 16. APRIL 1949 ERREICHT ALS 12 941 TONNEN NAHRUNGSMITTEL, KOHLE UND MEDIKAMENTE HAUPTSAECHLICH VON AMERIKANISCHEN „SKYMASTER" UND BRITISCHEN „YORK" FLUGZEUGEN NACH BERLIN GEFLOGEN WURDEN.

BERLIN AIRLIFT VETERAN

THIS „SKYMASTER" WAS ONE OF 205 AMERICAN C AIRCRAFT WHICH PROVIDED MOST OF THE UNITED CONTRIBUTION TO THE BRITISH, AMERICAN AND AIRLIFT INTO GATOW, TEMPELHOF AND TEGEL AIR DURING THE BLOCKADE OF BERLIN FROM JUNE TO MAI 1949. THE RECORD AIRLIFT FOR ONE D ESTABLISHED ON 16 APRIL 1949, WHEN 12 941 T FOOD, COAL AND MEDICINE WERE FLOWN TO BER PRIMARILY BY AMERICAN „SKYMASTERS" AND B YORKS.

Above: Workers of the Transportation Corp of the Berlin Military Post unload the last transport of the Berlin airlift. It was a C–54 Skymaster 45–510 piloted by Lieutenant Joe Russo from Chicago, Illinois. The transport and its cargo arrived at Tempelhof at 8.30p.m. on 30 September 1949, and the US First Airlift Task Force was deactivated on 1 October. (*Landesbildstelle–Berlin*)

Right: Scene at Rhein-Main air base on 12 May 1949 with personnel greeting a US Navy Douglas R5D– Skymaster from VR–6 Squadron with the news that the blockade was over. After long-drawn-out negotiations between the Allied powers and the USSR, shortly after midnight on Thursday, 12 May 1949 the barriers for road, rail and barge traffic to Berlin were raised and for the first time in eleven months supplies arrived in the city by means other than air transport. (*Landesbildstelle–Berlin*)

Opposite Below: This Douglas C–54 Skymaster 45–557 c/n 36010, a Berlin airlift veteran, is now preserved at Tempelhof along with a Douglas C–47 Skytrain. The Skymaster was one of 205 of the type which contributed most of the tonnage into the city between June 1948 and May 1949. The record for one day was established on 16 April 1949 when 12,941 tons (13,148 tonnes) of food, coal and medicine were airlifted into Berlin by the Allies. (*Helga Mellman USAF*)

Right: On 29 July 1949 CALTF held a parade at Fassberg in commemoration of those who lost their lives in the humanitarian airlift operations. The photo shows three Hastings from Schleswigland – TG518 'B', TG536 'D', TG574 'L' – representing the three squadrons – Nos.47, 53 and 297 – with No.53 completing 537 sorties into Berlin with its Handley Page-built transports. (*R3534 MoD AHB*)

Below: After a flight from Austrialia covering some 6,500 nautical miles, Dakota ZD215 alias RAAF A65–69 lands at Gatow on 22 June 1980 piloted by Air Vice-Marshal David Evans RAAF, an airlift veteran. Also on board was Squadron Leader C.S. 'Dinny' Ryan who completed 240 trips on the airlift as a signaller, one of forty RAAF aircrew who flew RAF Dakotas from Lübeck. It was presented to the Berlin Airlift Memorial Museum by the Australian government. (*Peter J. Bish*)

Bottom: As a tribute to Berlin airlift aircraft and the many gallant aircrew who flew the RAF transports, RAF Gatow has a Hastings and a Dakota on permanent display. The Dakota was a gift from Australia and is A65–69 c/n 27127 which was flown in from RAF Gütersloh on 22 June 1980 after its long flight from Australia. Radio call-sign was 'MBKHG', and one of the pilots on its last leg was Air Vice-Marshal David Evans who as a young Flying Officer took part in the humanitarian airlift in 1948/49 as part of the Commonwealth air forces contribution. (*RAF Gatow*)

Above: The two workhorses involved in Operation 'Plainfare' are seen preserved and on display outside the huge terminal building at Tempelhof. Both were World War Two vintage which had served well in the Allied theatre of operations. The C–54 Skymaster, with a wingspan of 117ft 6in (35.8m), first flew on 14 February 1942, and the C–54M, stripped to carry coal, had a payload of 35,000lb (15,876kg). The ubiquitous C–47 Skytrain had a 95ft (29m) wingspan, first flew as the DC–3 on 17 December 1935, and could carry over 7,000lb (3,175kg) of cargo.
(*US Air Force*)

Below: The last 'Vittles' flight departed Rhein-Main air base on 30 September 1949 at 1845 hours. Sister C–54 Skymaster transports flew in formation to mark the end of a dramatic chapter in world air transport history. Figures hurriedly painted on the C–54 represented the total tonnage airlifted by US transports. The combined total tonnage was 2,325,509.6 tons (2,362,717.7 tonnes), a figure disputed in 1956 by the British Air Ministry who quoted 695 tons (706 tonnes) less.
(*US Air Force*)

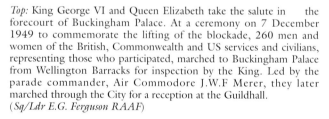

Top: King George VI and Queen Elizabeth take the salute in the forecourt of Buckingham Palace. At a ceremony on 7 December 1949 to commemorate the lifting of the blockade, 260 men and women of the British, Commonwealth and US services and civilians, representing those who participated, marched to Buckingham Palace from Wellington Barracks for inspection by the King. Led by the parade commander, Air Commodore J.W.F Merer, they later marched through the City for a reception at the Guildhall. (*Sq/Ldr E.G. Ferguson RAAF*)

Above: High-ranking personalities, service and civilian, representing the Allies take the salute on 29 July 1949 at the huge parade and flypast held at Fassberg in commemoration of those who lost their lives in the Berlin airlift. The photo shows personnel from the British Army, the Royal Air Force, the US Air Force and US Navy, the French military and a representative from the British civil air contribution. (*AP Photo Library*)

Right: The march in London on 7 December 1949 to Buckingham Palace from Wellington Barracks. (*AP Photo Library*)

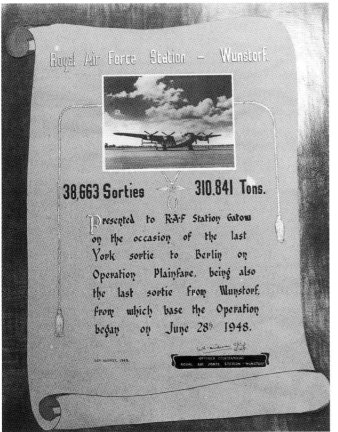

Above: After the ceremonial march through the City of London on 7 December 1949 a luncheon was held in the Guildhall hosted by the Lord Mayor. Among the many dignitaries present was Prime Minister Clement Attlee and Air Chief-Marshal Sir Arthur Tedder. The Allies and Commonwealth were well represented and included General William H. Tunner from the US Air Force.
(*Sq/Ldr E.G. Ferguson RAAF*)

Left: Dated 26 August 1949 this plaque was one of many produced by service units at the end of the airlift. Eight squadrons and one Operational Conversion Unit (OCU) of Avro Yorks provided transports for the airlift from the RAF, operating mainly out of RAF Wunstorf. Along with others this plaque was on display in the Officers' Mess at RAF Gatow.
(*RAF Gatow*)

Above: The scene outside Tempelhof airport on 11 July 1951 when the Berlin Airlift Memorial, a three-pronged white shaft arcing and flaring into the sky from a black basalt base, was unveiled. The names of those lost on the airlift are inscribed on the base. The memorial was designed by Professor Eduard Ludwig, a noted German architect.
(*USAF*)

Right: Operation 'Plainfare' plaque presented to RAF Gatow after the end of the airlift. It was a fine tribute to the ubiquitous Douglas Dakota and the Allied crews who operated the type. Although operating from a pool, the Dakota crews retained their squadron identity with pride, with no fewer then eight squadrons involved plus Commonwealth personnel from the RAAF, RNZAF and SAAF.
(*RAF Gatow*)

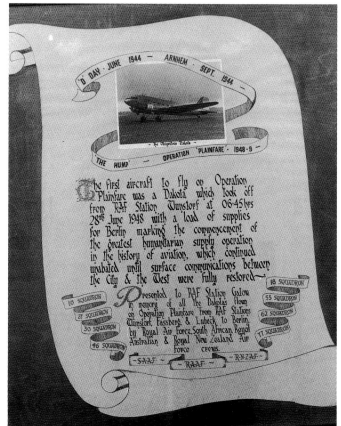

Above: The Berlin Airlift Memorial stands proudly in the Platz der Luftbrücke – Airbridge Square – adjacent to Tempelhof airport. In this photo some of the airport buildings and the airfield radar complex are visible. The memorial is 63ft (19m) high and 19ft (5.8m) wide at the base. The three prongs represent the three Allied powers who participated in the humanitarian airlift of 1948/49. (*USAF*)

Appendix 1

Operation 'Plainfare':
RAF units employed in support,
June 1948 – September 1949

No.10 Squadron – Douglas Dakota C IV*
No.18 Squadron – Douglas Dakota C IV
No.24 Squadron – Douglas Dakota C IV, Avro York C 1, Avro Lancastrian II
No.27 Squadron – Douglas Dakota C IV
No.30 Squadron – Douglas Dakota C IV
No.40 Squadron – Avro York C 1
No.46 Squadron – Douglas Dakota C IV
No.47 Squadron – Handley Page Hastings C 1
No.51 Squadron – Avro York C 1
No.53 Squadron – Dakota C IV, Handley Page Hastings C 1**
No.59 Squadron – Avro York C 1
No.62 Squadron – Douglas Dakota C IV
No.77 Squadron – Douglas Dakota C IV
No.99 Squadron – Avro York C 1
No.201 Squadron – Short Sunderland GR V
No.206 Squadron – Avro York C 1
No.230 Squadron – Short Sunderland GR V
No.238 Squadron – Douglas Dakota C IV***
No.242 Squadron – Avro York C 1
No.297 Squadron – Handley Page Hastings C 1
No.511 Squadron – Avro York C 1
No.235 Operational Conversion Unit – Short Sunderland GR V
No.240 Operational Conversion Unit – Douglas Dakota C IV
No.241 Operational Conversion Unit – Avro York C 1
No.114 (MEDME) Detachment – Douglas Dakota C IV

*   No.10 Squadron became effective in October 1948 when it absorbed No.238 Squadron.

**   No.53 Squadron was re-formed as a Hastings Squadron on 1 August 1949.

***   No.238 Squadron was renumbered No.10 Squadron in October 1948.

The first Handley Page Hastings arrived at Schleswigland in November 1948 with No.47 Squadron from RAF Dishforth, Yorkshire. No.24 Squadron was titled 'Commonwealth' Squadron with effect from April 1947, and after that it always had an element of aircrew personnel from the RAAF, RCAF and RNZAF.
    Although the Royal Canadian Air Force did not contribute Dakota crews for the airlift as did the RAAF, RNZAF and SAAF, personnel from the RCAF on aircrew exchange tours with No.24 'Commonwealth' Squadron did complete a number of airlift sorties with the squadron.

Appendix 2

Operation 'Plainfare':
Casualties

Royal Air Force casualties

York MW288 19 September 1948
Crashed at Wunstorf after engine failure following night take-off. All crew killed.

Crew:	175967	Flt Lt H. W. Thomson	–	Pilot
	166759	Flt Lt G. Kell	–	Co-Pilot
	1604758	Nav II L. E. H. Gilbert	–	Navigator
	1577861	Sig II S. M. L. Towersey	–	Signaller
	1881703	Eng II E. W. Watson	–	Flight Engineer

Dakota KP223 17 November 1948
Crashed at night inside the Russian Zone near Lübeck airfield when approaching to land in bad weather. Crew killed immediately except for Flt Lt Wilkins who died of his injuries later.

Crew:	1316810	Pilot 1 F. I. Trevona	–	Pilot
	55636	Flt Lt J. G. Wilkins	–	Navigator
	3001781	Sig III P. A. Lough	–	Signaller
	2221594	Sgt F. Dowling	–	Passenger

Dakota KN491 24 January 1949
Crashed at night inside the Russian Zone near Lübeck airfield when approaching to land in bad weather. Sgt Grout was killed and the other two members injured. In addition, seven German passengers were killed and a number of others injured.

Crew:	575250	Pilot II E. J. Eddy	–	Pilot
	1594259	Nav II L. Senior	–	Navigator
	1375129	Sig II L. E. Grout	–	Signaller

Dakota KJ970 22 March 1949
Crashed at night inside the Russian Zone near Lübeck airfield when approaching to land in bad weather. Crew killed immediately except for Sgt Penny who died of his injuries later.

Crew:	A412688	Flt Lt M. J. Quinn, RAAF	–	Pilot
	59342	Fg Off K. A. Reeves	–	Navigator
	552860	M Sig A. Penny	–	Signaller

Hastings TG611 16 July 1949
Crashed early morning at Tegel immediately after take-off. All crew killed.

Crew:	59756	Fg Off I. R. Donaldson	–	Pilot
	7597167	Sgt J. Toal, Glider Pilot Regt	–	Co-Pilot
	1324598	Nav I W. G. Page	–	Navigator
	1826137	Sig II A. Dunsire	–	Signaller
	5030958	Eng II R. R. Gibbs	–	Flight Engineer

Appendix 3

Operation 'Vittles':
Order of Battle, December 1948

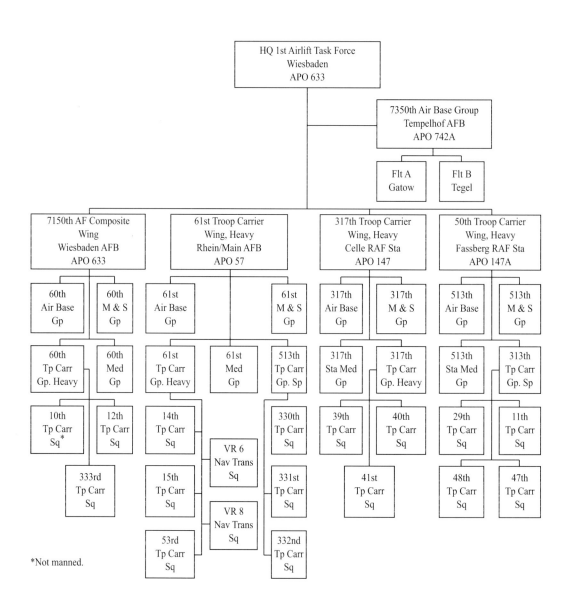

HQ 1st Airlift Task Force
Wiesbaden
APO 633

7350th Air Base Group
Tempelhof AFB
APO 742A

Flt A Gatow

Flt B Tegel

7150th AF Composite Wing
Wiesbaden AFB
APO 633

61st Troop Carrier Wing, Heavy
Rhein/Main AFB
APO 57

317th Troop Carrier Wing, Heavy
Celle RAF Sta
APO 147

50th Troop Carrier Wing, Heavy
Fassberg RAF Sta
APO 147A

60th Air Base Gp

60th M & S Gp

61st Air Base Gp

61st M & S Gp

317th Air Base Gp

317th M & S Gp

513th Air Base Gp

513th M & S Gp

60th Tp Carr Gp. Heavy

60th Med Gp

61st Tp Carr Gp. Heavy

61st Med Gp

513th Tp Carr Gp. Sp

317th Sta Med Gp

317th Tp Carr Gp. Heavy

513th Sta Med Gp

313th Tp Carr Gp. Sp

10th Tp Carr Sq*

12th Tp Carr Sq

14th Tp Carr Sq

330th Tp Carr Sq

39th Tp Carr Sq

40th Tp Carr Sq

29th Tp Carr Sq

11th Tp Carr Sq

333rd Tp Carr Sq

VR 6 Nav Trans Sq

15th Tp Carr Sq

331st Tp Carr Sq

41st Tp Carr Sq

48th Tp Carr Sq

47th Tp Carr Sq

VR 8 Nav Trans Sq

53rd Tp Carr Sq

332nd Tp Carr Sq

*Not manned.

122

Appendix 4

Monthly tonnages

Month	US		British		Total	
	Flights	Tonnages	Flights	Tonnages	Flights	Tonnages
26 June–31st July 1948	8117	41,188	5,919	29,053	14,036	70,241
August	9,796	73,632	8,252	45,002	18,048	118,634
September	12,905	101,871	6,682	36,556	19,587	138,427
October	12,139	115,793	5,943	31,245	18,082	147,038
November	9,046	87,963	4,305	24,629	13,351	112,592
December	11,655	114,572	4,834	26,884	16,489	141,456
January 1949	14,089	139,223	5,396	32,739	19,485	171,962
February	12,051	120,404	5,043	31,846	17,094	152,250
March	15,530	154,480	6,627	41,686	22,157	196,166
April	19,129	189,972	6,896	45,405	26,025	235,377
May	19,365	192,247	8,352	58,547	27,717	250,794
June	18,451	182,722	8,049	57,602	26,500	240,324

A USAF Douglas C-54 Skymaster as seen being refuelled at Rhein-Main air base near Frankfurt after the transport had arrived back from a delivery of vital supplies to the beleagured city of Berlin. All credit must go to the maintenance crews who nursed the four Pratt & Whitney R-2000 series Twin Wasp air-cooled engines which powered each Skymaster. Take-off rating was listed as 1,450 hp. (*Douglas*)

Appendix 5

Civil Airlift:
Organisation Chart

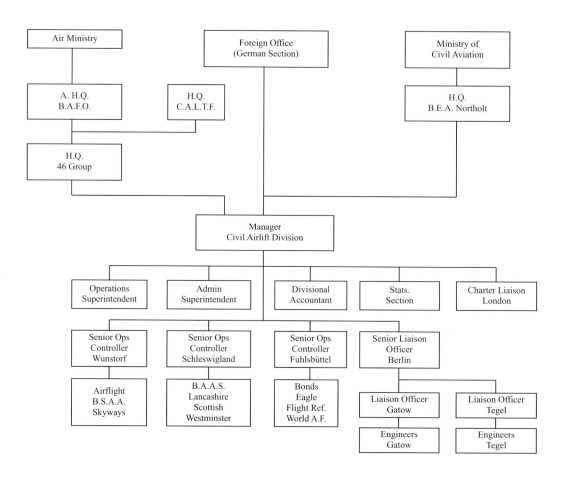

Appendix 6

Civil Airlift:
Individual aircraft performances

| Aircraft | | Freighter | | | Tanker | | | Total | | |
Type	Reg'n	Sorties	Hours	Tonnage	Sorties	Hours	Tonnage	Sorties	Hours	Tonnage
Air Contractors										
Dakota	G–AIWC	172	466.44	613.5	–	–	–	172	466.44	613.5
	G–AIWD	53	154.35	192.4	–	–	–	53	154.35	192.4
	G–AIWE	161	445.30	570.7	–	–	–	161	445.30	570.7
	Total	386	1,066.49	1,376.6	–	–	–	386	1,066.49	1,376.6
Airflight										
Tudor	G–AGRY	85	299.24	749.1	421	1,165.51	3,658.7	506	1,464.75	4,407.8
	G–AKBY	–	–	–	415	1,156.14	3,575.8	415	1,156.14	3,575.8
Lincoln	G–ALPF	1	2.49	7.1	45	115.11	425.9	46	117.60	433.0
	Total	86	232.13	756.2	881	2,437.16	7,660.4	967	2,669.29	8,4166
Airwork										
Bristol										
Freighter	G–AHJD	58	174.32	290.6	–	–	–	58	174.32	290.6
	G–AICS	16	44.12	80.0	–	–	–	16	44.12	80.0
	Total	74	218.44	370.6	–	–	–	74	218.44	370.6
Air Transport										
(CI) Dakota	G–AIVZ	205	562.10	742.6	–	–	–	205	562.10	742.6
Aquila										
Airways Hythe	G–AGER	6	19.45	32.6	–	–	–	6	19.45	32.6
	G–AGIA	118	322.34	632.3	–	–	–	118	322.34	632.3
	G–AHEO	141	358.19	744.3	–	–	–	141	358.19	744.3
	Total	265	699.98	1,409.2	–	–	–	265	6.99.98	1,409.2

Night loading scene at RAF Honington, Suffolk with a Rolls-Royce Merlin engine for an Avro York transport being manoeuvred with some difficulty into Dakota KN274 G for George. Aircraft tyres are waiting nearby to be loaded prior to a night flight to Germany. Fortunately the Douglas workhorse was available to the RAF in large numbers, nearly 2,000 being delivered under Lend-Lease agreement during World War Two. (*R2105 MoD AHB*).

British American Air Services										
Halton	G–AIAR*	–	–	–	247	789.16	1,805.5	247	789.16	1,805.5
	G–AKBB	48	119.13	237.1	25	86.42	149.8	73	205.55	386.9
	G–AKGN	49	114.03	287.7	292	876.44	1,982.8	341	990.47	2,270.5
	Total	97	233.16	524.8	564	1,752.42	3,938.1	661	1,985.58	4,462.9
British Nederland Air Services										
Dakota	G–AJZX	76	230.03	276.4	–	–	–	76	230.03	276.4
British South American Airways										
Tudor	G–AKBZ	–	–	–	517	1,423.12	4,391.9	517	1,423.12	4,391.9
	G–AGRH	114	322.13	1,134.2	–	–	–	114	322.13	1,134.2
	G–AGRJ	117	319.22	1,178.2	–	–	–	117	319.22	1,178.2
	G–AKCA	–	–	–	529	1,432.32	4,480.9	529	1,432.32	4,480.9
	G–AKCB	–	–	–	454	1,229.23	3,832.4	454	1,229.23	3,832.4
	G–AKCC	–	–	–	446	1,211.29	3,818.8	446	1,211.29	3,818.8
	G–AKCD	–	–	–	385	1,035.12	3,288.8	385	1,035.12	3,288.8
	Total	231	641.35	2,312.4	2,331	6,331.08	19,8128	2,562	6,972,43	22,125.2
British Overseas Airways Corporation										
Dakota	G–AGIZ	21	58.11	76.2	–	–	–	21	58.11	76.2
	G–AGNG	33	89.38	119.8	–	–	–	33	89.38	119.8
	G–AGNK	27	76.21	98.0	–	–	–	27	76.21	98.0
	Total	81	223.70	294.0	–	–	–	81	223.70	294.0
Bond Air Services										
Halton	G–AHDN	139	391.55	757.2	–	–	–	139	391.55	757.2
	G–AHDO	295	670.27	2,089.2	–	–	–	295	670.27	2,089.2
	G–AHDP	243	591.03	1,354.4	–	–	–	243	591.03	1,354.4
	G–AHDS	436	997.14	2,833.1	–	–	–	436	997.14	2,833.1
	G–AHDT	70	291.26	384.8	–	–	–	70	291.26	384.8
	G–AHDU	363	854.28	2,505.1	–	–	–	363	854.28	2,505.1
	G–AHDW	65	235.44	357.5	–	–	–	65	235.44	357.5
	G–AHDX	180	621.16	1,092.3	–	–	–	180	621.16	1,092.3
	G–AIOI	129	305.32	877.7	–	–	–	129	305.32	877.7
	G–AIWN	292	646.08	2,189.4	–	–	–	292	646.08	2,189.4
	G–ALON	204	458.08	1,489.3	–	–	–	204	458.08	1,489.3
	G–ALOS	161	362.27	1,201.4	–	–	–	161	362.27	1,201.4
	Total	2,577	6,423.88	17,131.4	–	–	–	2,577	6,423.88	17,131.4
Ciros Aviation										
Dakota	G–AIJD	91	268.48	330.9	–	–	–	91	268.48	330.9
	G–AKJN	237	661.39	846.5	–	–	–	237	661.39	846.5
	Total	328	929.87	1,177.4	–	–	–	328	929.87	1,177.4
Eagle Aviation										
Halton	G–AIAP	390	885.23	2,727.8	–	–	–	390	885.23	2,727.8
	G–AIAR†	60	132.25	432.0	–	–	–	60	132.25	432.0
	G–ALEF	227	545.27	1,481.4	–	–	–	227	545.27	1,481.4
	G–AJBL	377	907.47	2,662.6	–	–	–	377	907.47	2,662.6
	Total	1,054	2,470.22	7,303.8	–	–	–	1,054	2,470.22	7,303.8
Flight Refuelling										
Lancastrian	G–AGWI	–	–	–	226	579.14	1,381.0	226	579.14	1,381.0
	G–AGWL	–	–	–	361	881.25	2,422.6	361	881.25	2,422.6
	G–AHJU	–	–	–	438	1,175.59	2,429.1	438	1,175.59	2,429.1
	G–AHJW	–	–	–	40	130.20	221.0	40	130.20	221.0
	G–AHVN	–	–	–	279	657.28	1,586.1	279	657.28	1,586.1
	G–AKDO	–	–	–	431	1,141.02	2,683.0	431	1,141.02	2,683.0
	G–AKDP	–	–	–	378	1,053.53	2,216.9	378	1,053.53	2,216.9
	G–AKDR	–	–	–	526	1,472.04	3,070.1	526	1,472.04	3,070.1
	G–AKDS	–	–	–	480	1,305.31	2,784.5	480	1,305.31	2,784.5

	G–AKFF	–	–	–	449	1,129.14	3,022.5	449	1,129.14	3,022.5
	G–AKFG	–	–	–	439	1,099.38	2,943.0	439	1,099.38	2,943.0
	G–AKTB	–	–	–	391	985.33	2,354.8	391	985.33	2,354.8
	Total	–	–	–	4,438	11,609.21	27,114.6	4,438	11,609.21	27,114.6
Hornton Airways Dakota	G–AKLL	108	301.25	397.5	–	–	–	108	301.25	397.5
Kearsley Airways Dakota	G–AKAR	84	234.35	301.6	–	–	–	84	234.35	301.6
	G–AKDT	162	445.22	587.0	–	–	–	162	445.22	587.0
	Total	246	679.57	888.6	–	–	–	246	679.57	888.6
Lancashire Aircraft Corporation Halton	G–ALCX	–	–	–	151	481.52	873.4	151	481.52	873.4
	G–AHWN	78	237.41	492.4	230	793.03	1,345.3	308	1030.44	1,837.7
	G–AHYH	–	–	–	313	1,007.20	1,827.5	313	1,007.20	1,827.5
	G–AIHV	–	–	–	282	886.29	1,640.6	282	886.29	1,640.6
	G–AIHY	26	63.35	178.6	180	585.04	1,285.5	206	648.39	1,464.1
	G–AILO	–	–	–	98	312.20	583.9	98	312.20	583.9
	G–AJZY	–	–	–	228	733.04	1,282.7	228	733.04	1,282.7
	G–AJZZ	–	–	–	89	273.45	493.5	89	273.45	493.5
	G–AKBJ	–	–	–	195	645.38	1,138.7	195	645.38	1,138.7
	G–AKBK	–	–	–	289	905.10	1,709.5	289	905.10	1,709.5
	G–AKEC	79	220.57	544.3	80	257.11	488.6	159	477.68	1,032.9
	G–AKXT	–	–	–	242	733.03	1,358.0	242	733.03	1,358.0
	G–ALBZ	–	–	–	200	633.41	1,170.7	200	633.41	1,170.7
	Total	183	522.13	1,215.3	2,577	8,193.40	15,197.9	2,760	8.767.13	16.413.2
Scottish Airlines Dakota	G–AGWS	51	126.29	175.9	–	–	–	51	126.29	175.9
	G–AGZF	50	127.45	172.2	–	–	–	50	127.45	172.2
Liberator	G–AHDY	–	–	–	233	733.52	1,534.0	233	733.52	1,534.0
	G–AHZP	15	36.42	110.1	–	–	–	15	36.42	110.1
	G–AHZR	–	–	–	148	489.21	1,182.5	148	489.21	1,182.5
	Total	116	290.16	458.2	381	1,222.73	2,716.5	497	1,512.89	3,174.7
Silver City Airways Bristol Freighter	G–AGVB	65	199.21	292.3	–	–	–	65	199.21	292.3
	G–AGVC	73	210.00	324.4	–	–	–	73	210.00	324.4
Bristol Wayfarer	G–AHJC	38	105.23	141.7	–	–	–	38	105.23	141.7
	G–AHJO	37	105.07	138.0	–	–	–	37	105.07	138.0
	Total	213	619.51	896.4	–	–	–	213	619.51	896.4
Sivewright Airways Dakota	G–AKAY	32	87.06	116.1	–	–	–	32	87.06	116.1
Skyflight Halton	G–AIWP	16	44.21	106.7	–	–	–	16	44.21	106.7
	G–AKBR	24	61.22	169.4	–	–	–	24	61.22	169.4
	Total	40	105.43	276.1	–	–	–	40	105.43	276.1
Skyways York	G–ALBX	467	1,279.16	4,616.6	–	–	–	467	1,279.16	4,616.6
	G–AHFI	147	411.29	1,364.3	–	–	–	147	411.29	1,364.3
	G–AHLV	467	1,259.43	4,194.2	13	38.44	108.8	480	1,297.87	4,303.0
Lancastrian	G–AHBT	–	–	–	459	1,229.02	3,437.6	459	1,229.02	3,437.6
	G–AKFH	–	–	–	196	507.55	1,675.9	196	507.55	1,675.9
	G–AKMW	–	–	–	479	1,265.17	3,600.7	479	1,265.17	3,600.7
	G–AKSN	–	–	–	228	590.45	1,950.2	228	590.45	1,950.2
	G–AKSO	–	–	–	293	766.05	2,540.0	293	766.05	2,540.0
	Total	1,081	2,949.88	10,175.1	1,668	4,397.48	13,313.2	2,749	7,347.36	23,488.3

Transworld Charter Viking	G–AHON	37	101.47	130.3	–	–	–	37	101.47	130.3
	G–AHOT	81	220.59	285.1	–	–	–	81	220.59	285.1
	Total	118	322.46	415.4	–	–	–	118	322.46	415.4
Trent Valley Aviation Dakota	G–AJPF	186	504.25	665.5	–	–	–	186	504.25	665.5
World Air Freight Halton	G–AKAC	255	602.26	1,776.4	–	–	–	225	602.26	1,776.4
	G–AKGZ	7	16.25	45.0	–	–	–	7	16.25	45.0
	G–AITC	264	593.45	1,881.8	–	–	–	264	593.45	1,881.8
	Total	526	1,212.36	3,703.2	–	–	–	526	1,212.36	3,703.2
Westminster Airways Dakota	G–AJAY	44	127.10	159.7	–	–	–	44	127.10	159.7
	G–AJAZ	184	527.55	664.3	–	–	–	184	527.55	664.3
Halton	G–AHDL	–	–	–	10	33.45	64.4	10	33.45	64.4
	G–AHDM	176	450.35	928.0	106	351.25	815.7	282	801.06	1,743.7
	G–AHDV	–	–	–	136	455.50	824.5	136	455.50	824.5
	G–AJNW	–	–	–	116	367.48	887.3	116	367.48	887.3
	Total	404	1,105.40	1,752.0	368	1,208.48	2,591.9	772	2,313.88	4,343.9
Grand total (All aircraft)		8,713	22,630.81	54,634.8	13,208	37,151.96	92,345.4	21,921	59,782.77	146,980.2

*This aircraft hired out to Eagle Aviation is a freighter after completion of tanker duties with BAAS.

†This aircraft hired from BAAS

Appendix 7

Civil Dakota Statistics for the Berlin Airlift

Contractor	Reg.	Sorties	Flying Time	Dates
Air Contractors	C–AIWC	172	466.44	4 Aug 48–10 Nov 48
	G–AIWD	53	154.35	
	G–AIWE	161	445.30	
Air Transport Charter	G–AJVZ	205	562.10	4 Aug 48–10 Nov 48
British Nederland Air Services	G–AJZX	76	230.03	21 Sept 48–14 Nov 48
B.O.A.C.	G–AGIZ	21	58.11	21 Oct 48–25 Nov 48
	G–AGNG	33	89.38	
	G–AGNK	27	76.21	
Ciros Aviation	G–AIJD	91	268.48	6 Aug 48–10 Nov 48
	G–AKJN	237	661.39	
Horton Airways	G–AKLL	108	301.25	24 Sept 48–18 Nov 48
Kearsley Airways	G–AKAR	84	234.35	4 Aug 48–20 Nov 48
	G–AKDT	162	445.22	
Scottish Airlines	G–AGWS	51	126.29	4 Aug 48–27 Aug 48
	G–AGZF	50	127.45	
Sivewright Airways	G–AKAY	32	87.06	19 Oct 48–15 Nov 48
Trent Valley Aviation	G–AJPF	186	504.25	4 Aug 48–10 Nov 48
Westminster Airways	G–AJAY	44	127.10	4 Aug 48–23 Nov 48
	G–AJAZ	184	527.55	

Appendix 8

Civil Airlift:
Casualties

Lancastrian G–AHJW
Flight Refuelling Limited, 23 November 1948

Capt Cyril Taylor
Capt Reginald Merrick Watson Heath
Capt William Cusack
Nav Off Michael Edwin Casey
Nav Off Alan John Burton
Rad Off Dornford Winston Robertson
Flt Eng Kenneth Arthur Seaborne

Aircraft accident at Thruxton, England

Accident with a RAF Hastings
Lancashire Aircraft Corporation, 15 January 1949

Gd Eng Theodor Supernatt
Gd Eng Patrick James Griffin
Gd Eng Edward O'Neil

Ground accident at Schleswigland, Germany; one German killed also.

York G–AHFI
Skyways Limited, 15 March 1949

Capt Cecil Golding
First Off Henry Thomas Newman
Rad Off Peter James Edwards

Aircraft accident at Gatow, Berlin, Germany.

Halton G–AJZZ
Lancashire Aircraft Corporation, 21 March 1949

Capt Robert John Freight
Nav Off James Patrick Lewin Sharp
Eng Off Henry Patterson

Aircraft accident at Schleswigland, Germany

Halton G–AKAC
World Air Freight, 30 April 1949

Capt William Richard Donald Lewis
Nav Off Edward Ernest Carroll
Eng Off John Anderson
Rad Off Kenneth George Wood

Aircraft accident 20 miles from Tegel, Berlin.

Appendix 9

Berlin Airlift

Public Record Office,
Ruskin Avenue, Kew, Richmond, Surrey TW9 4DU.
Tel: 0181-876-3444.
Opening hours 9.30 to 5.00 Monday to Friday.

Operation 'Plainfare'

The single most important document on Operation 'Plainfare' is to be found in AIR 10/5067. This is a large Air Publication, No.3257, entitled 'A report on Operation Plainfare (the Berlin Airlift)' by Air Marshal T.M. Williams, C-in-C of BAFO, dated April 1950. The report is so comprehensive that it was decided in the 1950s that an official narrative was not required. However, those wishing to do additional work should look also at Berlin Airlift Progress Reports contained in AIR 8/1647–1650, 1658. Other interesting examples of 'Plainfare' material include AIR 20/7148 Operation 'Plainfare' (1948–1951); AIR 20/7071 Air Supply of Berlin: Civilian Aviation Contribution (1948–1949); and AIR 15/816–817 Coastal Command Activities: Operation 'Plainfare' (1948–1949). An interesting post-airlift file is AIR 8/1855 Berlin – Air Safety Talks with Russians (1953–1954).

Appendix 10

AIRLIFT FOUNDATIONS
AND ASSOCIATIONS

Luftbrücke Chapter of the Airlift/Tanker Association

Located at Rhein-Main air base, Germany, the Luftbrücke Chapter of the Airlift/Tanker Association seeks to maintain the symbolic importance of the Berlin airlift and to treasure the memories of seventy-nine freedom fighters who died in the humanitarian operation of 1948/49. The association is a tax-free non-profit group which is sponsoring the development of the Berlin Airlift Memorial. Initial realisation of the memorial was accomplished for DM 900,000 and was financed by friends of the memorial, enthusiastic sponsors like American Airlines, the Frankfurt Commercial Airport, AFN TV-Guide, companies located in the United States and Germany, as well as individuals.

The monument is an exact replica of the Berlin Airlift Memorial located at Berlin's Tempelhof Airport which was designed by Professor E. Ludwig. The Frankfurt monument is located close to the main gate entrance to Rhein-Main air base and is dedicated to the seventy-nine American, British, French and German personnel who died in the airlift. The steel and concrete monument is floodlit twenty-four hours a day, and is used as a beacon for both ground and air traffic. It symbolises the western end of a 'bridge' with the monument in Berlin. It is flanked by two examples of the type of aircraft which actually flew with the US Forces on the airlift from Rhein-Main, a Douglas C–47 Skytrain and a Douglas C–54 Skymaster. Surrounding the monument is a beautifully landscaped park and rose garden including a wooded area.

The Berlin Airlift Memorial complex is located adjacent to the main north–south, west–east *autobahn* through Europe. The visitors centre with museum, now in the planning phase overseen by the Frankfurt Commercial Airport, will be located in the former Officers' and NCO Club building and the area around. Once it is completed, this whole complex promises to be another significant tourist attraction. The Berlin Airlift Memorial/Luftbrücke Chapter will get office space and an area in which to display memorabilia etc. in the new visitors centre, enabling the Berlin Airlift/Luftbrücke Chapter to operate from there and remain active, with many interesting functions and programmes for the public.

The Luftbrücke Chapter is one of thirty chapters belonging to the Airlift/Tanker Association, which comprises approximately 3,000 members, mainly located in the United States. Gerdi and Gerhard Rausch are executive directors of the Berlin Airlift Memorial/Luftbrücke Chapter at Rhein-Main air base, 60549 Frankfurt/Main, Germany.

Berlin Airlift Historical Foundation

Founded in 1988 the foundation is a non-profit, tax exempt corporation which meets the charitable requirements of Section 501 of the US Internal Revenue Code. It has a membership of both general and associate members, veterans of the airlift, historians, educators and patriots located in Great Britain, the USA, France and Germany.

The foundation's claim to fame is that in December 1992 it purchased a Douglas C–54E Skymaster transport which it named *Spirit of Freedom*, and today it functions as a flying museum, airlift memorial and classroom. It is registered N500EJ. During 1996 alone the Skymaster attended no fewer than twenty-one venues in the USA. It received two awards, the first being at the famous EAA Annual Air Show at Oshkosh for best cargo transport. At the Berlin Airlift Veterans Association reunion it received the American Spirit Award. It is planned to fly the C–54 to Berlin for the 50th Anniversary celebrations of the ending of the humanitarian operation on 12 May 1999.

The foundation had originally planned to purchase a Douglas C–47 Skytrain (Dakota) as its second aircraft, but an opportunity came to obtain a rare Boeing C–97 Stratofreighter which took priority. It is a C–97G N117GA ex-52–2718 and named *Deliverance*. It was a single YC–97A 46–59595 which joined the Berlin airlift briefly on 2 May 1949 flying its first mercy trip to Berlin two days later. The C–97G N117GA has only 8,000 hours on the airframe and had been used for humanitarian relief flights throughout Central and South America. The foundation board of directors voted 100 per cent in favour of the purchase on 13 March 1996 and the purchase agreement was signed on 22 April. The new transport will be a flying history book and will present events involving the Cold War in Europe from the airlift in 1948 to the removal of the Berlin Wall in 1988. Appropriate display panels will be mounted in the fuselage along with a variety of memorabilia etc. The acquisition of a Douglas C–47 is now for the future, but once procured it will be finished in RAF Transport Command markings as a tribute to Great Britain's and the RAF's role in the airlift. With some 1,000 still flying around the globe, the purchase of a suitable Skytrain/Dakota should not prove difficult.

All these projects need support and funding. Current worldwide supporting membership for the foundation exceeds 500, centred around what they term the 'Spirit of Freedom National Support Group for the C–54, C–97 and eventually the C–47'. Founder and president of the foundation is Timothy A. Chopp, PO Box 782, Farmingdale, New Jersey 07727, USA.

British Berlin Airlift Association.

After three airlift veterans – Alan Smith, Max Chivers and Tommy Trinder – attended the nostalgic closure ceremony including farewell parade at RAF Gatow on 11 May 1994, the decision to form a British Berlin Airlift Association was taken. Early in September 1994 after ten airlift veterans from RAF Dakota and York squadrons, together with ten airlift veterans from the USA, had the honour of being invited by the Berlin Senate to attend the military ceremonies in Berlin on 6/7/8 September 1994 marking the withdrawal of the Western Allies from the city, its existence was assured.

Today it is possibly one of the most active ex-service associations in the United Kingdom with membership fringing on 500, and it is governed and guided by a strong and enthusiastic committee. The requirement for membership is simply to have been engaged either directly or indirectly in the huge humanitarian operation. All three British services were involved, plus many civilians including those from the British civil aviation charter companies and airlines that took part. At least two newsletters are issued annually, and periodically an updated list of members is issued. A long weekend reunion is held each spring, this now absorbing the all important AGM, an annual formal dinner with guests, and includes a visit to an aeronautical establishment or an active RAF base. The 1996 weekend was located in Peterborough involving a visit to the Imperial War Museum collection at Duxford. Telford in Shropshire was the venue for the 1997 weekend, this being located near the huge RAF Aerospace Museum at Cosford. The taking over of a hotel for the weekend enables members, wives and guests to socialise. An autumn meeting is held annually during September at the Victory Services Club in London, the highlight being the luncheon, which is always well attended. The first AGM and lunch was held at the RAF Club in Piccadilly during September 1995 when well over 200 members and guests attended including German TV and representatives from the Airlift Gratitude Foundation in Berlin. The association retains close links with this foundation and also with the two active airlift associations in the USA.

The president of the BBAA is Air Chief-Marshal Sir Nigel Maynard KCB CBE DFC AFC who commanded No.242 Squadron Yorks during the airlift; Vice-president is Air Marshal Sir John Curtiss KCB KBE FRAeS CBIM, ex-navigator on No.59 Squadron Yorks. The very active working committee is headed by Alan D. B. Smith who flew on the airlift as a Flight Lieutenant flight engineer on Yorks, being a member of the RAF Transport Command Development Unit – TCDU – with a crew who were seconded to No.99 Squadron. He was subsequently given pilot training and became a Squadron Leader, later becoming a training captain with British Airways. Secretary and treasurer is ex-Squadron Leader Frank Stillwell, an airlift navigator on No.30 Squadron Dakotas; assistant secretary is John Collier, ex-RAF Regiment at Wunstorf; while the excellent newsletter editor and PRO is Geoff W. Smith, ex-electrician at RAF Gatow. Finally, association supplies officer is Squadron Leader Peter Izard RAFVR, ex AQM with No.51 Squadron on Yorks.

Associate membership is available to persons not directly involved with the humanitarian airlift of 1948/49, such as widows of airlift personnel and airlift historians. Address for secretary: 9 Barnards Hill, Marlow, Bucks SL7 2NX.

The Airlift Gratitude Foundation

Ten years after the end of the airlift in 1949, the mayor of Berlin, Willy Brandt, and the president of the Berlin House of Representatives, Willy Henneberg, announced in the name of the Berlin government a scheme to raise funds for the bereaved of the airlift. In the first two months DM 1,626,000 was raised. On 25 August 1959 the official establishment of the foundation by the Berlin government followed. The foundation charter read:

> In memory of the sacrifices made by the American, English, French and German people during the Berlin blockade through the establishment of the airlift in the period from 28 June 1948 to 30 September 1949, a foundation is to be created by the City of Berlin from funds contributed in gratitude for the airlift . . . Its goal is to express the ties between Berlin and the airlift nations.

During the first ten years of its existence, the foundation almost exclusively devoted its efforts to supporting dependants of the victims, offering either a lump sum or monthly payments; in several cases the request for a visit to Berlin was financed or a gift was given. Particular emphasis was placed on the education of the children, and in several cases the foundation made higher education or university studies possible. In many cases the extra expenses of boarding schools were handled by the organisation. Up to 1997 four airlift widows, including one American, received continuous support from the foundation at a rate constantly adjusted to meet cost-of-living increases. Between 1959 and 1995 the foundation granted dependants of the victims more than two million Deutschmarks in aid, helping eighty-eight individuals.

The aid to dependants of the fallen airlift casualties constitutes only a small portion of the original mission. In close co-operation with the German Academic Exchange Service (DAAD) and the Technical and Free University of Berlin, it was possible to award a total of more than 200 fellowships between 1965 and 1997. In addition to students and scholars, a number of artists were supported. The Airlift Gratitude Foundation, or Stiftung Luftbrückendank, provided a total of DM 3.2 million through 1995 for academic grants.

Director of the foundation is Heinz–Gerd Reese whose office is located at the Berliner Rathaus, D–10173 Berlin.

South African Air Force Berlin Airlift Reunion Committee

Surviving members of the SAAF who flew on the Berlin airlift are kept in touch by the Berlin Airlift Reunion Committee whose chairman is Major-General D.M. Ralston SD SM FSAIAeE, with an annual reunion each October.

It is not generally known that the SAAF contributed two contingents to the humanitarian operation, and in addition had aircrew serving on secondment with No.24 'Commonwealth' Squadron in the United Kingdom, making a total of no fewer than eighty-one personnel. Some thirty plus are surviving and active with the organisation. Unfortunately two – Lt Janse van Rensberg and Lt P. Norman-Smith – were later killed in action in the Korean conflict.

Lt J.F. van Rhyneveld is the son of the founder of the South African Air Force, General Sir Pierre van Rhyneveld. Lt T. Condon was awarded the Air Force Cross (AFC) after an engine cut out on his Dakota while on short finals into Gatow at night. He was forced to go round again, fully loaded with coal, when the GCA lost the aircraft on their scope at low level due to a thunderstorm.

The late Colonel P.M.J. McGregor corresponded with the author and submitted his airlift experiences with a copy of the item he had published in the July 1949 edition of the *South African Air Force Journal*. Address: PO Box 12251, Clubview 0014, South Africa.

Berlin Airlift Veterans Association

The Berlin Airlift Veterans' Association was established in Las Vegas, Nevada, USA, in September 1990. Since that time it has held yearly reunions in various cities throughout the US and in 1994 returned to Germany to celebrate the 45th Anniversary of the humanitarian airlift.

The Association has dedicated a plaque at the Airlift Memorial located at Rhein-Main Air Base, Germany, and others at Scott AFB and Wright Patterson AFB in the USA. During September 1997 the Association held a dedication ceremony at the US Air Force Academy in Colorado. In 1998 it is planned to dedicate a tablet and a tree at Arlington National Cemetery in Washington DC.

Members of the Association have given many talks to various groups of people and are well received at these functions. The Association is continually looking for new members by publishing stories of the historic airlift in various newspapers and magazines.

Secretary/Treasurer is Bill Gross, BAVA, 7616 Upper Sequin Road, Converse Texas 78109, USA.

Most of the British civil Dakotas employed on the airlift were ex RAF, as were many of the aircrew who flew them. Standardisation with the type assisted greatly in many ways including flight procedures. Depicted is G-AKLL of Horton Airways which, between 24 September and 18 November 1948, completed 108 sorties into Berlin airlifting nearly 400 tons (406.5 tonnes) of vital supplies. (*Aviation Photo News*).

Production of the Avro York for the RAF amounted to 208, which included 114 pure freighters and 64 passengers/freighters. On the airlift the York carried an average of nine tons (9.15 tonnes) of supplies, completed 29,000 sorties and carried a total of 230,000 tons (233,703 tonnes) into Berlin. RAF Wunstorf was the German base used by the Yorks and here the vital task of refuelling is shown. The refuelling bowser takes the 100 octane fuel, known as AVGAS to the transport.

(Inset) Fuel being fed into the wing of an Avro York at Wunstorf. (*MoD AHB*).

Diary of Events

June 1948

11   All Allied and German railroad freight traffic between the Western zones and Berlin suspended by the Russians for two days.

16   Soviets walk out of Allied Kommandatura meeting in Berlin.

17   Plan prepared by HQ BAFO for supply of British troop garrison in Berlin by air under Operation 'Knicker'

24   All surface communications with Berlin halted.

25   First eight RAF Dakotas arrive at Wunstorf – others followed.

26   Airlift begins. Thirty-two flights by USAFE Douglas C–47 Skytrains carry eighty tons of supplies from Wiesbaden to Tempelhof. US airlift named Operation 'Vittles'.

28   Operation 'Knicker' put into full operation. At 0600 hrs first Dakota took off from Wunstorf for Gatow. During the following twenty-four hours thirteen Dakotas airlifted forty-four tons of food to Berlin. First thirty-five Douglas C–54 Skymasters en route to Germany from Alaska, Hawaii, the USA and the Caribbean. Brig-Gen Joseph Smith assigned command of airlift by Lt-Gen Curtis LeMay, Commander USAFE.

30   RAF operation re-named 'Carter Patterson'. USAF Wiesbaden utilising eighty C–47s. First C–54 Skymasters arrive 9.30a.m., first leaves for Tempelhof at 7.36p.m.

July

1   Avro Yorks of the RAF Transport Command flown from UK bases to Wunstorf. Russians withdraw completely from Berlin Allied Kommandatura.

3   Yorks commence airlifting goods to Gatow – dehydrated potatoes.

5   Two squadrons of RAF Sunderland flying boats join airlift. Operating from Finkenwerder on the River Elbe to Havel Lake, Berlin.

7   First coal flown into Gatow by RAF Dakotas. Airlift exceeds 1,000 tons (1,016 tonnes) in twenty-four hours.

9   First fatal accident on airlift near Wiesbaden. Two C–47 pilots and one US Department of the Army civilian employee killed.

10   HQ British Army Air Transport Organisation moved to the Schloss, Bückeburg, leaving RASO at Wunstorf and FASO at Gatow.

12   Construction commenced on new runway at Tempelhof.

16   Concrete runway at Gatow completed.

19   British airlift operation re-named Operation 'Plainfare' American Overseas Airlines (AOA) commenced twice-daily flights between Frankfurt and Tempelhof with Douglas DC–3s.

20   Gen Lucius D. Clay flies to Washington for airlift discussions with President Truman. Total of 2,250 tons (2,286 tonnes) airlifted into Berlin in twenty-four-hour period by RAF and USAF. Airlift aircraft strength reaches fifty-four C–54s, one hundred and five C–47s, forty Yorks, fifty Dakotas.

23   HQ USAF directs MATS (Military Air Transport Service) to establish provisional Task Force HQ, with Maj-Gen William H. Tunner to command under the control of USAFE. HQ USAF directs MATS to provide maintenance facilities and traffic personnel for eight additional squadrons of nine C–54 Skymasters each.

25   Second fatal aircraft crash when USAF C–47 crashes in Berlin on apartment house in Friedenau borough. Crew of two killed.

27   Russians threaten to fly in twenty-mile-wide corridors to Berlin. Gen Tunner and advance party leave USA for Wiesbaden. Flight Refuelling commenced airlift operation from Bückeburg with three Avro Lancastrian tanker aircraft.

29   RAF Dakotas transferred from Wunstorf to Fassberg. Gen Tunner and advance party arrive in Wiesbaden.

30   Two additional squadrons of C–54 Skymasters arrive. New airlift daily record – 1,918 tons flown by USAF.

31   In 339 flights, airlift hauls exactly 2,027 tons (2,059.43 tonnes).

August

3   Two further MATS squadrons of C–54s leave USA for Germany.

4   New record for USAF – 2,104 tons (2,138 tonnes). First day of British civil airlift. One Halton (Bond), one Liberator (Scottish Airlines) operate out of Wunstorf. Nine civil Dakotas operating out of Fassberg. Two Hythe flying boats (Aquila) operating out of Finkenwerder.

5   Huge USAF air base at Oberpfaffenhofen near Munich designated as maintenance depot for USAF 'Vittles' aircraft for 200-hr inspection. First grass sod cut on site of new airfield at Tegel, in French sector of Berlin. First Berlin manufactured goods flown out to Western zones.

6   Ciros Aviation position one Dakota at Fassberg.

7   Combined airlift sets new record with 666 flights, airlifting 3,800 tons (3,860 tonnes).

8   Third flight of two MATS C–54 squadrons depart USA for Germany. Flight Refuelling move to Wunstorf.

10   Remaining flights of two C–54 squadrons depart Japan and Hawaii for Germany. New record lift – 2,437 tons (2,476 tonnes), 346 flights.

12   In 707 flights USAF and RAF deliver 4,742 tons (4,818 tonnes), first above daily average of 4,500 tons (4,572 tonnes) estimated necessary to keep the Berliners alive.

13   Fiftieth day for airlift. Gen Tunner demands revised flights pattern and requests experienced air traffic controllers from USA after experiencing hazardous stacking conditions with aircraft over Tempelhof. Black Friday.

14   Scottish Airlines Liberator withdrawn from airlift. First Douglas C–74 Globemaster I transport arrives in Germany from USA carrying eighteen spare C–54 engines weighing 38,000lb (17,237kg).

15   First ten-ton cargo of newsprint since blockade inception flown to Berlin.

17   Douglas C–74 makes first internal airlift flight, hauling twenty tons of flour into Gatow. This is twice the C–54 payload.

20   RAF Dakota squadrons commence move to Lübeck from Fassberg.

21   Three squadrons of USAF C–54 Skymasters move into Fassberg, operating into Gatow with coal. 'Little Vittles' inaugurated by Lt Gail S. Halvorsen by dropping sweets to Berlin children on approach to Tempelhof.

24   Four USAF aircrew killed in mid-air crash of two C–47s in thick fog over Ravolzhausen. New USAF record – 3,030 tons (3,078 tonnes) delivered in 395 flights.

26   Eagle join airlift with one Halton operating out of Wunstorf. Total tonnage delivered to Berlin by USAF passed 100,000 mark.

27   Scottish Airlines Dakota withdrawn.

28   All civil aircraft based at Fassberg moved to Lübeck.

31   New daily record by USAF – 3,124 tons (3,174

tonnes) carried.

September

1   Work commenced at Burtonwood air depot, Lancashire, to replace Oberpfaffenhofen as maintenance depot for airlift C–54 aircraft. German civilians, including women, employed at Tegel number 19,000.

2   First twenty US civilian air traffic controllers, demanded by Gen Tunner, join airlift.

3   Airflight arrive at Wunstorf with Tudor freighter.

9   USAF record – 3,392 tons (3,446 tonnes).

10   USAF record – 3,527 tons (3,583 tonnes).

13   First three of five twin-engined Fairchild C–82 Packets or 'Flying Boxcars' arrive at Wiesbaden to supplement airlift.

15   Arrival of RAAF Dakota aircrews at Lübeck.

17   Halton freighters of Skyflight commence flying from Wunstorf.

18   US Air Force (Europe) celebrates US Air Force Day by hauling record load 6,987.7 tons (7,100 tonnes) to Berlin. Special coal bonus distributed to Berliners. Approximately 15,000 German guests visit USAF bases at Wiesbaden and Rhein-Main. Silver City join airlift using two Bristol Wayfarers operating out of Wunstorf.

19   First fatal RAF crash. Five aircrew killed when Avro York MW288 crashed on take-off at Wunstorf.

21   British Nederland Air Service position one Dakota at Lübeck. First contingent of SAAF Dakota aircrew depart South Africa for UK, then Germany. Arrive Oakington, Cambridgeshire, 26th.

23   British South American Airways (BSAA) commence operating from Wunstorf with two Tudor Is, while Transworld Charter commence operations with one Viking.

24   The Douglas C–74 Globemaster I makes last of twenty-four flights to Berlin delivering a total tonnage of 428.6 (435 tonnes). Dakota of Horton Airways arrives at Lübeck.

26   Test flights into Berlin by Tudor tanker aircraft with diesel oil.

30   Douglas C–47 Skytrains of USAFE withdrawn from airlift.

October

1   1/Lt John Finn from Jackson, Michigan, becomes first USAF pilot to complete 100 airlift missions. Aircrew training for airlift C–54 aircrews established at Great Falls, Montana, USA.

2   Fire truck collides with C–54 Skymaster at Rhein-Main. One killed.

4   United Nations Security Council in New York commence discussing the Berlin blockade by the USSR.

5   All British civilian aircraft based at Lübeck moved to Fuhlsbüttel, Hamburg.

6   World Air Freight commence flying from Wunstorf with one Halton. Skyflight withdrawn from airlift.

7   Notification by HQ RAF Transport Command of decision to operate new Handley Page Hastings aircraft on airlift.

8   World Air Freight Halton G–AKGZ crashed at Gatow – no casualties.

14 Allied airlift efforts combined under one operational HQ. Maj-Gen William H. Tunner appointed Commanding General of Combined Airlift Task Force (CALTF) with Air Commodore John Merer RAF as deputy. The 1,000th C–54 Skymaster flight on airlift out of Wiesbaden.

15 Lt-Gen John K. Cannon takes over as Commanding General of USAFE.

16 Lancashire Aircraft Corp. position three Halton freighters at Wunstorf.

17 Total of 454 short tons (554 tonnes) flown into Gatow in twenty-four-hour period by British aircraft.

18 First fatal C–54 Skymaster crash. Three USAF aircrew died in dense forest area four miles from Rhein-Main. USAF recalls 10,000 ex-pilots, radio operators and flight engineers for active airlift duty in Europe.

19 The backloading of German civilians from Gatow to Lübeck by RAF Dakotas commenced. Sivewright Airways joined airlift at Hamburg with one Dakota.

20 BOAC position three Dakotas at Hamburg.

21 President Truman directs USAF to augment airlift with up to sixty-six more C–54 Skymasters after conference at the White House with Gen Clay.

26 Russia rejects UN Security Council resolution to terminate blockade. Arrival of RNZAF aircrew at Lübeck.

28 Airflight Tudor freighters converted to tankers.

29 Tegel dedicated in ceremonies to mark opening of Berlin's third airlift terminal.

30 Lancashire Aircraft Corp. operated Halton tankers from Wunstorf.

November

1   First squadron – No.47 – Hastings arrived at Schleswigland.

3   The 300,000th short ton flown into Berlin by CALTF aircraft.

5   Operations commence at Tegel. The 300,000th ton flown into Berlin was by a C–54 piloted by 1/Lt Donald G. Bidwell from Dayton, Ohio, USA.

8   Secretary of State for Air, Arthur Henderson, arrived in Germany from UK for tour of RAF airlift bases. First three of twenty-four US Navy Douglas R5D–Skymaster transports arrive for airlift duty.

10 Trent Valley, Ciros, Air Contractors and Kearsley Airways withdrawn from airlift. Airwork positioned Bristol Freighter at Hamburg.

11 First Hastings transport operated on airlift.

14 Two Vikings and British Nederland Dakota withdrawn from airlift, Bond Air Services moved Haltons from Wunstorf to Hamburg.

15 Sivewright and Air Transport (C.I.) withdrawn from airlift. Final transfer by air of maintenance crews from Oberpfaffenhofen to Burtonwood. Regular C–54 maintenance scheduled for 18th start.

16 Airlift aircraft experience first test of winter weather, continuing normal operations despite heavy fog. Skyways joined airlift at Wunstorf with three Yorks.

17 A USAF radar team departs Westover AFB, Massachusetts, for Germany to commence installation and flight trials of new CPS–5 radar in the control tower at Tempelhof. RAF Dakota KP223 crashed at night in Russian Zone near Lübeck. Three aircrew killed, one survivor died later in hospital.

18 The first RAF Dakota KN446 from 30 Squadron at Lübeck piloted by Sq Ldr A.M. Johnstone flew into Tegel the new airfield in the French sector of Berlin. Hornton Airways withdrawn from airlift.

21 Tudor tankers of British South American Airways (BSAA) commenced operation from Wunstorf.

22 The 500,000th short ton flown into Berlin by CALTF aircraft.

23 Westminster Dakotas withdrawn from airlift. Flight Refuelling Lancastrian G–AHJW crashed at Thruxton, UK. Seven killed.

25 US Thanksgiving Day celebrated by USAF and US Navy with airlift of 6,116 tons (6,214 tonnes).

26 Thick fog conditions hamper airlift operations. GCA in extensive use for landings. Gatow recorded 1,316 in one month. Backlog in Berlin reported as just one month's food. All civilian Dakotas withdrawn from airlift.

29   BSAA withdraw one Tudor freighter.

December

1   USAF weather observation/reconnaissance squadron commenced flights over North Atlantic and through the Berlin corridors. Equipped with Boeing WB–29 Superfortress aircraft.

5   Construction of a second runway – 2,300 yds (2,103m) – commenced at Tegel.

6   USAF C–54 Skymaster crashes on take-off from Fassberg. Crew of three killed.

7   Weather improves, fog lifts, operations normal.

8   Capt Utting, chief pilot of Airflight, knocked down and killed by truck on the tarmac at Gatow.

9   Combined Allied airlift delivers 6,133 tons (6,231 tonnes), second highest. Silver City position two Bristol Freighters at Hamburg.

11   US Navy R5D– Skymaster with six on board crashes in Taunus mountains. Crew chief killed. British American Air Services commence flying with Haltons from Hamburg.

13   171st day of airlift. Total tonnage delivered by CALTF – 640,284 (650,529 tonnes). US tonnage 460,501 (467,870 tonnes); British tonnage 179,783 (182,660 tonnes).

15   All RAF Sunderlands and civil Hythe flying boats withdrawn from airlift due to threat of ice on Havel Lake. Finkenwerder closed. 317th Troop Carrier Group with C–54 Skymasters moves from Wiesbaden to Celle, opening second US airlift terminal in British Zone.

16   French Army engineers blow up transmitting towers of communist-controlled broadcasting station in immediate vicinity of Tegel. USAF announced that airlift C–54 Skymasters will be increased to 225 by end of December. Lancashire Aircraft Corp. ceased to operate freighters – only tankers. 5,000th landing by civil aircraft made by Skyways York. Total load carried to date by civil aircraft on airlift now over 26,170 tons (26,589 tonnes).

20   Fassberg flies in gifts for 10,000 Berlin children in Operation 'Santa Claus'.

24   World Air Freight positioned one Halton freighter at Hamburg.

25   The 50,000th landing by an airlift aircraft at Gatow made by RAF Dakota from Lübeck.

26   A total of 700,172.7 (711,375 tonnes) tons airlifted into Berlin in 96,640 flights over six months.

31   Airlift completes 100,000 flights by Allies to Berlin since operations began.

January 1949

1   Highest weekly total to date of 41,287 short tons (41,948 tonnes) flown by CALTF. Liquid fuel target for January by civil airlift – diesel 145 short tons (147 tonnes); petroleum 75 tons (76 tonnes), daily.

2   First Skyways Lancastrian tanker arrived at Wunstorf.

7   USAF C–54 Skymaster crashes north of Burtonwood, Lancashire. Six killed.

8   BSAA withdraw second Tudor I aircraft from airlift.

13   Airlift establishes record, second only to US Air Force Day, by flying 6,678.9 (6,786 tonnes) tons to Berlin in 755 flights.

14   USAF C–54 Skymaster crashed near Rhein-Main. Three killed.

15   Tegel opened to civil aircraft. Three Lancashire Aircraft Corp. ground engineers plus one German killed in accident involving RAF Hastings at Schleswigland.

17   Weekly record of 41,540 tons (42,205 tonnes) achieved.

18   USAF C–54 Skymaster crashes ten miles east of Fassberg. Pilot killed.

19   750,000th short ton (762,000 tonnes) delivered to Berlin by CALTF.

24   250,000th ton (254,000 tonne) of coal arrives at Tegel from Fassberg. RAF Dakota KN491 crashed at night in Russian Zone near Lübeck. Wireless operator and seven German passengers killed.

25   British American Air Services converted Halton freighter to tanker and commenced operations from Schleswigland.

31   Highest monthly total to date lifted by CALTF – 171,960 short tons (174,711 tonnes).

February

1   Liquid fuel target for month by civil airlift: 245 tons (249 tonnes) of diesel, petrol and kerosene daily.

3   Highest tonnage to date in twenty-four-hour airlift by British aircraft – 1,736 short tons (1,764 tonnes) in 293 sorties.

5   Silver City withdrawn from airlift.

12   Airwork withdrawn from airlift.

15   Air Ministry decision not to re-employ flying boats on the airlift.

18   The 1,000,000th ton (1,016,000 tonnes) of supplies by CALTF reaches Berlin, flown in by RAF York.

19   Scottish Airlines rejoin airlift with two Liberator tankers from Schleswigland.

20 Weather reduces airlift to 205.5 tons (209 tonnes) in twenty-two flights. 200th day of British civil airlift.

26 8,025 tons (8,153 tonnes) in 902 flights makes all-time airlift tonnage record. Top weekly tonnage record of 44,612 tons (45,326 tonnes).

March

1 Liquid fuel target for month – 350 tons (356 tonnes) daily.

4 Prime Minister Clement Attlee arrives at Bückeburg to commence visit of airlift bases and facilities.

11 The RAF flew to Lübeck from Gatow the 50,000th German civilian.

15 HQ No.46 Group RAF Transport Command moved from Bückeburg to Luneberg.

16 USAFE reveal that from 1 July 1948 to 1 March 1949 US aircraft have accomplished 36,797 landings by GCA radar.

21 Lancashire Aircraft Corp. Halton G–AJZZ crashed near Schleswigland. Crew of three killed.

22 RAF Dakota KJ970 crashed at night inside the Russian Zone near Lübeck. Pilot and navigator killed; signaller died later.

31 Highest monthly tonnage to date lifted by CALTF – 196,160.7 (199,300 tonnes). 61st Maintenance Squadron, Rhein-Main, claims new USAF record for 154 engines rebuilt during month of March. US Navy Squadron VR–8 sets an all-time record of 155 per cent efficiency, with hourly utilisation of 12.2 hours per Skymaster.

April

1 Liquid fuel target for month – 350 tons (356 tonnes) daily. Transfer of HQ No.46 Group from RAF Transport Command to BAFO. Civil Airlift Division (BEA) formed in Berlin.

7 Tempelhof GCA radar crews handle 102 aircraft at a rate of one every four minutes over a six-and-a-half-hour period to set up a new high in sustained operation. Fassberg C–54 Skymaster completes entire round trip to Berlin in 1hr 57min; turnaround time 15min 30sec.

11 Highest tonnage to date in twenty-four hours lifted by CALTF – 8,246 short tons (8,378 tonnes) in 922 sorties. RAF and British civil aircraft from Wunstorf contributed 1,135 short tons (1,153 tonnes), the highest total to date from that base.

16 Flight Refuelling move from Wunstorf to Hamburg. Gen Tunner's 'Easter Parade' effort flies 12,940 tons (13,147 tonnes) of coal, food and other supplies in 1,398 flights to raise 24-hr operation record to new high; 3,946 take-offs and landings made, plus 39,640 radio contacts – one every four seconds during the 24-hr watch period. Eighty per cent of the aircraft involved remained in commission, with many units maintaining a 100 per cent utilisation during most of the period. British contribution to this effort was 2,035 short tons (2,068 tonnes) airlifted.

21 300th day of blockade. 927 transports airlift 6,393.8 tons (6,496 tonnes). Work commences on third runway at Gatow.

23 Third-high single-day tonnage – 8,774.3 tons (8,915 tonnes) in 974 flights. New weekly tonnage figure: 58,155.8 tons (59,086 tonnes) in 6,437 flights.

25 Tass news agency reveals the Russian willingness to lift the blockade. New second-high figure: 8,939.1 tons (9,082 tonnes) in 1,011 flights.

26 US State Department reveals Jessup–Malik talks and says 'way appears clear' for lifting blockade.

27 Another second-high record: 9,119.9 tons (9,266 tonnes) in 1,022 flights.

30 World Air Freight Halton G–AKAC crashed north of Tegel in Russian Zone. Four crew killed. Highest monthly tonnage to date lifted by CALTF – 232,267 short tons (235,983 tonnes). This marks a daily average of 7,845.5 tons (7,910 tonnes) during the month. New weekly record of 60,774.2 tons (61,747 tonnes) of food and supplies.

May

1 Civil Airlift Division joins HQ No.46 Group at Lüneberg. Liquid fuel target for the month – 550 tons (559 tonnes) daily.

2 Boeing YC-97A Stratofreighter joins the airlift arriving at Rhein-Main.

4 YC–97 airlifts its first ten-ton load to Templehof. Big Four delegates announce Berlin blockade would be lifted on 12 May.

7 British Foreign Secretary Ernest Bevin arrives in Berlin to inspect airlift installations.

9 Highest British tonnage in twenty-four-hour period flown into Berlin – 2,167 short tons (2,202 tonnes).

10 Flight Refuelling Lancastrian G–AKDP force-landed in Russian Zone. No casualties. 9,257 tons (9,405 tonnes) carried. 1,019 flights to establish new second high.

12 The Berlin blockade was lifted at 0001 hrs. Rail lines and highways to the city re-opened. Highest British tonnage in period – 2,183 short tons (2,218 tonnes).

14   Secretary of State for Air arrived at Wunstorf on visit to airlift bases and installations.

15   New weekly high of 61,749.9 tons (62,738 tonnes).

22   British civil airlift record day – 1,009 short tons (1,025 tonnes) in 132 sorties.

31   Tonnage airlifted by CALTF during month – 250,818 short tons (254,831 tonnes). Airflight Tudors withdrawn from airlift. 100,000th ton delivered to Berlin by civil airlift.

June

1   Liquid fuel target for month – 550 tons (559 tonnes) daily. The 100,000th short ton of liquid fuel flown into Berlin by a British civil Lancastrian from Fuhlsbüttel, Hamburg. Rotation scheme for RAF squadrons commenced.

8   Airlift includes daily haul of eight tons of first class mail.

18   Fassberg stages 'Blockade Busters Party' with over 3,000 US and UK personnel.

19   Skyways York G–ALBX crashed near Wunstorf. No casualties.

24   Airflight Avro Lincoln tanker arrived at Wunstorf.

26   First anniversary of US airlift. 8,944 tons (9,087 tonnes) delivered. Skyways Lancastrian G–AKFH burnt out at Gatow. No casualties. Previous British tonnage record again passed – 2,244 short tons (2,280 tonnes) in twenty-four hours.

28   First anniversary of British airlift.

30   Highest daily total by RAF and civil aircraft – 2,263 short tons (2,299 tonnes) in twenty-four hours.

July

2   The two millionth short ton delivered by CALTF flown into Berlin by USAF C–54 Skymaster.

4   US Independence Day. 9,374.5 tons (9,525 tonnes) delivered.

12   Rundown of British civil airlift commenced. Airflight Lincoln withdrawn from airlift. British American Air Services, Lancashire, Scottish, Westminster ceased to operate. Schleswigland closed to civil operations.

13   Liquid fuel target reduced to 140 tons (142 tonnes) daily.

17   Skyways Lancastrian tankers withdrawn.

21   British element of CALTF delivered its 500,000th short ton (508,000 tonnes).

24   Military government in Berlin reports an average of eighty-eight days' foodstuff stockpiled in the city.

29   Huge CALTF parade held at Fassberg in commemoration of those who lost their lives in the airlift.

August

1   US airlift element officially terminated and begins rundown of units after 400 consecutive days. Rundown of RAF operation commenced. USAF operations from Celle ceased.

10   Flight Refuelling and British South American Airways withdrawn from airlift.

12   British civil airlift operations from Fühlsbuttel ceased.

15   Bond Air Services, Eagle Aviation, World Air Freight withdrawn. Skyways withdrawn from Wunstorf and operations ceased.

16   End of the British civil airlift. Last charter aircraft withdrawn.

22   Night flying on the airlift ceased.

29   RAF York squadrons ceased operations.

September

1   HQ CALTF disbanded. USAF operations from Fassberg ceased. Tegel closed.

23   RAF Dakota squadrons ceased to operate on airlift.

30   Last flight to Berlin with USAF C–54 Skymaster in Operation 'Vittles' – 17,835,727th ton (18,121,098 tonnes).

October

6   RAF Hastings ceased to operate.

15   HQ No.46 Group closed at Lüneberg, and numberplate transferred back to RAF Transport Command.

Author's note: This diary of events was compiled from at least four published chronology items which have appeared over the years. It is therefore inevitable that some of the facts and figures, and even dates, conflict with the data published in the manuscript. However, for the first time the airlift events covering the entire Allied effort, including the civil contribution, have been recorded together.

Bibliography

Arnold-Forster, Mark, *The Siege of Berlin* (Collins, 1979).

Barker, Dudley, *Berlin Air Lift* (HMSO, 1949).

Collier, Richard, *Bridge Across the Sky* (McGraw-Hill, 1978).

Ferguson, Aldon P., *Burtonwood* (Airfield Publications, 1985); *Royal Air Force Burtonwood* (Airfield Publications, 1989).

Giangreco, D.M. and Griffin,Robert E., *Airbridge to Berlin* (Presidio Press, 1987).

Jackson, Robert, *The Berlin Airlift* (Patrick Stephens, 1988).

Kidson, Philip, *Avro on the Airlift* (A.V. Roe & Co. Ltd).

Miller, R.E., *A Bridge Yesterday* (RAF Gatow, 1994).

Morris, Eric, *Blockade – Berlin & the Cold War* (The Military Book Society, 1973).

Pearcy, Arthur, *The Dakota* (Ian Allan, 1972); 'Berlin Airlift' (*Aviation News* Vol. 8 No.5); *The Berlin Airlift* (Flugzeug, 1988).

Reese, Heinze-Gerd, Schroder, Michael, and Schwarzkopf, Manfred, *Blockade & Airlift. Legend or Lesson?* (Airlift Gratitude Foundation, 1988).

Rodrigo, Robert, *Berlin Airlift* (Cassell & Co., 1960).

Steijger, Cees, *A History of USAFE* (Airlife, 1991).

Tunner, William H., *Over the Hump* (Office of Air Force History, 1964).

Tusa, Ann & John, *The Berlin Blockade* (Hodder & Stoughton 1988)

Wood, P.R., *The Berlin Airlift* (Air Clues, May 1979 MoD(AHB).

Miscellaneous publications

Civil Airlift – Operation Plainfare (1949).

Gilfillan Historical Feature (July 1987).

'Airlift to Berlin' (*National Geographic*, May 1949).

The Berlin Airlift – GCA Operation during 'Operation Vittles' (Airways & Air Communications Services USAF, June 1949).

Airlift Routes & Procedures (HQ CALTF 1948) CALTF Manual 60–1.

The Berlin Airlift (Data Package, March 1979).

N.B. This is by no means a complete listing of books and publications covering the Berlin airlift, only a list of those held by the author and used in conjunction with the research necessary for the production of this volume.